IN THE
HIGHEST
TRADITIONS
OF THE
ROYAL NAVY

To my wife, Julia Ryan Wills, the bravest person I have known.

And to the memory of my father Jesse Ely Wills who sowed the seed for this book on my seventeenth birthday by giving me a thin volume by Captain Russell Grenfell RN, entitled *The Bismarck Episode*.

IN THE HIGHEST TRADITIONS OF THE ROYAL NAVY

THE LIFE OF CAPTAIN JOHN LEACH MVO DSO

MATTHEW B. WILLS

FOREWORD BY ADMIRAL SIR JOCK SLATER GCB LVO DL
EDITED BY LIEUTENANT COMMANDER DOUGLAS HADLER RN

SPELLMOUNT

First published 2011
by Spellmount, an imprint of
The History Press
The Mill, Brimscombe Port
Stroud, Gloucestershire, GL5 2QG
www.thehistorypress.co.uk

British Library Cataloguing in Publication Data.
A catalogue record for this book is available from the British Library.

ISBN 978 0 7524 5992 9

Typesetting and origination by The History Press
Printed in Malta

CONTENTS

ACKNOWLEDGEMENTS

I wish to acknowledge the gracious permission of Her Majesty Queen Elizabeth II to use two quotations from the diary of King George VI, her father, which appear at the end of Chapter VIII.

I am forever grateful to all those who have helped me to write this book. More than anyone my father, Jesse Ely Wills, encouraged my enthusiasm for the Royal Navy during my formative years. In 1940 he began buying the current edition of *Jane's Fighting Ships* founded in 1897 in London by Fred T. Jane. I was allowed to browse the pages of what was then the definitive reference book in the world on fighting ships. On page 36 of the 1941 edition of *Jane's* there is an impressive drawing of a battleship built by Cammell Laird & Co. Ltd at Birkenhead. It was my earliest encounter with HMS *Prince of Wales*. Later my father encouraged me to read the works of C.S. Forester with their stirring accounts of fictional Royal Navy Captain Horatio Hornblower. My admiration for the Royal Navy soared. On my seventeenth birthday he gave me a slender book by Captain Russell Grenfell RN entitled *The Bismarck Episode*. It occupies a special place in my library and is among my most cherished possessions. On page 53 of Grenfell's book there is an unforgettable account of a 15-inch shell hitting the bridge of HMS *Prince of Wales*. It was my introduction to Captain John C. Leach.

I do not have a naval background from the standpoint of service; however, through my wife, Julia, I am blessed with family connections to two graduates of the United States Naval Academy at Annapolis. One is Julia's father, Commander Philip H. Ryan, whom I knew for almost 25 years. The other is Julia's brother, Ensign Philip H. Ryan Jr, a man I only knew through Julia's eyes. Both were true Virginia gentlemen and both were officers and gentlemen in the best traditions of the US Navy. Ensign Ryan's life was cut tragically short. On 3 August 1956, in the skies over the Naval Air Station at Corpus Christi, Texas, Philip's T32 jet trainer collided with another aircraft. Philip and his flight instructor both ejected. Philip did not survive. The flight instructor lived, but could never bring himself to communicate with Philip's parents or his sister. The examples of these two naval officers have given me a deep appreciation of the commitment and sacrifice that are expected of Annapolis graduates and all those who have passed out of Britannia Royal Naval College, Dartmouth.

On 25 January 2008 I wrote to Admiral of the Fleet Sir Henry Leach, GCB, DL to inform him that I was considering the possibility of writing a book about his distinguished father. Some may feel that I was presumptuous for a number of reasons: I am not British; I am not an academic historian; I do not have a naval background. Sir Henry was undismayed. On the contrary, he has helped me in every conceivable way. Amongst other things, he has shared his father's scrapbooks, letters and photographs. He has provided me with copies of his father's confidential reports, which the Royal Navy never releases to anyone except next of kin. Sir Henry has patiently answered a thousand and one written questions and after I had completed a rough draft of the manuscript, he went over it with me, page by page, correcting errors and suggesting various points that needed clarification. While Sir Henry has extended every courtesy to me that I could ever want, he has never in the least infringed on my prerogative to write this book in the light of historical truth as I have gleaned it. I am forever grateful to him. I am also grateful to Admiral Sir Jock Slater, GCB, LVO, DL, who generously offered to write the Foreword after reading the manuscript.

The research that went into this book is difficult to quantify; I could never have done it alone. For many months Lieutenant Commander Douglas Hadler has been my principal researcher in the UK. He has proven himself a conscientious and resourceful researcher and possesses tactfulness that far exceeds my own. In his case it has opened doors that may well have been closed to me. I will always be grateful to Douglas for his research.

Both Douglas Hadler and I have received kindness and encouragement from the vast majority of the individuals whom we have contacted in England. I wish to acknowledge the following for their help or their interest: Liza Verity, Information Specialist with the National Maritime Museum; Lieutenant Commander Brian Witts MBE, Curator HMS *Excellent* Museum; the late Dr. Colin S. White FSA FR HistS RNR, late Director of Royal Navy Museum; Captain C.L.W. Page MA C Eng FlMech E Royal Navy, Head of the Naval Historical Branch (Naval Staff) Ministry of Defence; R.W.A. Suddaby, The Keeper of the Department of Documents, Imperial War Museum; Ian D. Proctor, Curator, Photograph Archive, Imperial War Museum; S.J. Offord, Archive Assistant, Department of Documents, Imperial War Museum; Miss Pamela Clark, Registrar, The Royal Archives, The Round Tower, Windsor Castle.

Two individuals at Britannia Royal Naval College, Dartmouth, have been both gracious and helpful. Dr Jane E. Harrold is Archivist and Deputy Curator of Britannia Museum. She spent untold hours searching old issues of *Britannia Magazine* for information on Cadet John C. Leach's academic and athletic achievements. Richard Kennell is the erstwhile distinguished librarian for Britannia Royal Naval College, a position he held for over 30 years. Without any introduction I recently rang him up and rather presumptuously asked him if he would look up the precise wording of a famous quotation by a great figure from the College's past. He readily consented to do so. I wish to thank Mr Kennell for his kindness and I contritely apologise for my brashness.

Captain John A. Coiner, US Navy (Rtd) graduated from Annapolis a few years ahead of Julia's brother, Philip. He has provided me with detailed information on the movements of USS *Augusta* on her China Station in the period 1936–38. In those years *Augusta* had frequent contact with HMS *Cumberland*; their captains undoubtedly knew one another. The British captain was John C. Leach. Jack Coiner also discussed with me a tradition of both the US Navy and the Royal Navy of which until very recently I had been unaware, that at sea in naval vessels of destroyer/frigate size and above the captain ordinarily dines alone. I wish to express my appreciation to Jack for his research and for his consistent willingness to help.

Many books that I have used as sources are out of print, some for decades. A large percentage of these books came from the UK. Two books were only available in Australia. Doug Clausen, who with his wife, Pam, owns an intriguing used and rare book store in Colorado Springs, has never failed to find the book that I had asked him to track down. I am grateful to Doug for his diligence on my behalf.

I want to express my deep appreciation to Donna Kwiatkowski for deciphering my hardly legible handwriting and for repeatedly typing revisions of my manuscript. She surely deserves an inscribed copy.

In the autumn of 2010 Douglas Hader took on the responsibility for becoming my editor and my chief liaison with The History Press. The key figure at The History Press is Shaun Barrington. I have admired Shaun from afar and suspect that he has done far more for me than most publishers ever do for their authors. Douglas Hader has proved to be indispensible in his new roles.

To my daughters, Carter, Aurelia and Ellen, I want to say that you have encouraged me more than you know. To our eight grandchildren, I want to say that each of you will receive an inscribed copy of this book and I hope that it will stimulate your interest in British history. One of our grandchildren, Miles, is already an Anglophile. He lives with his parents, Aurelia and Thaddeus, an older brother Stewart, and an older sister Jessie, in Saint Paul, Minnesota. On display in Miles's room are a large Union Jack, a photograph of Captain Leach and in a framed case a Royal Navy bosun's call with a silver chain, which was a gift to him from Admiral of the Fleet Sir Henry Leach.

To my wife, Julia, I want to say that this book is dedicated to you because you are the bravest person I have known and the mainstay of my life.

FOREWORD

When John Leach joined the Royal Navy in 1907, Admiral Jackie Fisher was at the helm as First Sea Lord and his remarkable influence was well established. He resolutely pushed through major naval reforms, which were to shape the life and career of the young cadet – modernising the Fleet, not least in promoting improvements in naval gunnery, advancing the use of the torpedo and overhauling training standards.

Fisher had also reorganised officer entry, so Cadet Leach had started his career at Osborne House on the Isle of Wight moving to the new Royal Naval College at Dartmouth two years later. Above the front entrance of the College engraved in stone are the immortal words:

IT IS ON THE NAVY UNDER THE GOOD PROVIDENCE OF GOD THAT OUR WEALTH PROSPERITY AND PEACE DEPEND

What greater inspiration could a young cadet have setting out on his chosen career?

The American author of this absorbing book has had a lifelong interest in the Royal Navy. From C.S. Forester to *Jane's Fighting Ships*, he devoured every detail. As a teenager he read about the sinking of the *Bismarck*, not least the key role played by HMS *Prince of Wales*. This was the action that was to spark Matt Wills' particular interest in her Captain,

John Leach, and his illustrious career and was to lead many years later to this biography after detailed research into his life and times. By drawing the strands together from many sources, the author has painted a stirring picture of that historic period from the run-up to the First World War to the early days of the Second World War, a period in which John Leach was an increasingly prominent participant.

Inevitably, the book majors on Captain Leach's last appointment in 1941, bringing the second great battleship of the King George V Class out from build and taking her into action before she was fully operational and worked up, his subsequent onerous duty in transporting the Prime Minister and the First Sea Lord across the Atlantic to Newfoundland to meet President Roosevelt, the final months when Churchill insisted on deploying the *Prince of Wales* and the *Repulse* to the Far East against the First Sea Lord's advice and the disaster that followed.

Many years later, Admiral of the Fleet Sir Henry Leach, who had been with his father a few nights before the *Prince of Wales* was lost under Japanese air attack in the South China Sea, wrote of one of Churchill's greatest blunders, the First Sea Lord's failure to insist on his professional opposition to the deployment with lack of air cover, the shambles of the higher command in Singapore and the final mishandling of the operation. This all led to the tragic and untimely death of John Leach whom Churchill himself described as 'a charming and lovable man and all that a British sailor should be'. Indeed he was a gallant officer who was clearly destined for high office and, throughout his distinguished career, represented the highest traditions of the Royal Navy.

Admiral Sir Jock Slater GCB LVO DL
First Sea Lord 1995–1998

PROLOGUE

John Catterall Leach dedicated his life to his country by nearly 30 years of distinguished service in the Royal Navy. The story of his last command as Captain of HMS *Prince of Wales* has been told. What has not been told is the story of Captain Leach's entire life, which from an early age was shaped by the highest traditions of the Royal Navy. The following verses by one of England's greatest poets epitomise the best of these traditions:

In all the waters that are Britain's walls
The seaman faced the issue as it falls
Against all Death that shatters and appals.

Often the issue is at touch and go
Between a few ships and a foreign foe,
How close the issue only seamen know.

Through fifty years of strain and overstrain
Within those precincts men have come to train
That Right may stand, that Britain may remain.

Well have they struggled both in peace and war,
Through grimmer tests than ought prepare them for,
To keep the Seven Seas and hold the shore.

Long may such Courage guard, such Wisdom guide
The men who sail all seas on every tide
To save the Queen,
That she may prosper, and Her realm abide.

This poem by John Masefield, the Poet Laureate, was penned for the fiftieth anniversary of Britannia Royal Naval College. Masefield was honouring the College, but in another sense he was honouring all those Royal Navy officers who made the ultimate sacrifice. Captain John Catterall Leach MVO, DSO, Royal Navy belongs to that immortal company.

The sea has formed the English character and the essential England is to be found in those who follow it. From blue waters they have learned mercifulness and a certain spacious tolerance for what does not affect their craft; and they have also learned – in the grimmest schools – precision and resolution. The sea endures no makeshifts. If a thing is not exactly right it will be vastly wrong. Discipline, courage and contempt for all that is pretentious and insincere are the teaching of the ocean and the elements – and they have been qualities in all ages of the British sailor.

John Buchan

CHAPTER I

THE EARLY YEARS

John Catterall Leach was born on 1 September 1894 at Clevedon, Somerset, the only son of Reverend and Mrs Charles Rothwell Leach. Clevedon was a tiny seaside resort on the Severn Estuary. It was, perhaps, best known for Clevedon Court, part of which was believed to be well over 500 years old. Stephen Lacey, the well-known garden writer, described Clevedon Court and its environs:

> This is an ancient habitation. Remains of a Roman dwelling have been uncovered here, and the Great Hall and Tower were already standing when Sir John de Clevedon built the present manor house with its erratic roofline, and thick buttressed walls c.1320.[1]

It is a safe assumption that other features of Clevedon held much more allure for Jack Leach as a young boy than did the cold, austere walls of Clevedon Court. Clevedon is located where two ranges of hills meet. One range extending north to Portishead slopes to steep cliffs along the shore. The footpaths that meandered through this range provided Jack with endless opportunities to explore, but the dominant feature of Clevedon was the sea. As a schoolboy he soon learned that the sea defined the British Isles and connected the British Empire; that the sea was a barrier to Britain's ancient foes. Indeed, this rudimentary knowledge of the sea's vital role in the life of his country was the beginning of his understanding of the Royal Navy's raison d'être.

In that era most British boys were intrigued by ships. Jack Leach was no exception and it can be said that his interest was more serious than most. The two largest ports on the Severn Estuary were Bristol and Cardiff. In the last years of the nineteenth century there were still plenty of sailing boats to be seen, but they were mainly privately owned yachts. The era of the British tea clipper, somewhat smaller but faster than the Yankee clipper, had already passed. Of all the British tea clippers, the most famous was *Cutty Sark*. This three-masted sailing ship was launched at Dumbarton, Dunbartonshire in 1869. She had a varied career as a commercial vessel before being converted into a training ship. She has been saved for posterity and is now in permanent dry dock at Greenwich. At some point in his childhood Jack Leach surely read about *Cutty Sark* and her journeys to the exotic Far East.

It goes without saying that Jack would have seen illustrations of HMS *Victory*, the most famous ship in the history of the Royal Navy. It is highly likely that he would have read a boy's life of Lord Horatio Nelson, the Royal Navy's greatest hero. John Keegan has written, 'The artefacts and memorials of sea power are warp to the woof of British life. HMS *Victory*, cocooned in her dry dock at Portsmouth, is an object as much visited by British schoolchildren as the manuscript of their constitution by American.'[2] It is likely that he was taken to Portsmouth just to see HMS *Victory*.

The ships that he saw most often were pleasure craft coming from Bristol and cargo ships out of Cardiff. Eventually Cardiff would be the largest port in the world for the export of coal. The first time in his life that Jack Leach saw a Royal Navy ship with her white ensign rippling in the breeze is unknown, but it would have made a lasting impression.

Dreadnought is a great name in the annals of the Royal Navy. There were nine Royal Navy ships that bore that name including the fifth *Dreadnaught*, a three-decker of 98 guns that fought with Nelson at Trafalgar. When she was completed in 1906 the sixth HMS *Dreadnought* represented the latest in battleship design and construction.

[She was] a British battleship of the early 20th century that established the pattern of the all-big-gun warship that dominated the world's navies for nearly 40 years. Completed in 1906 'the *Dreadnought*' had four propellers driven by steam turbines and displaced 21,845 tons. She was capable of a speed of 21 knots (24 miles per hour) and mounted ten 12-inch guns in five turrets.[3]

When *Dreadnought* was launched at Plymouth on 9 February 1906, Jack Leach was five months beyond his eleventh birthday. All of England knew that HMS *Dreadnought* would be launched that day. The First Sea Lord, Jackie Fisher, planned an elaborate celebration to which he invited King Edward VII. The excitement and exaltation of that day have been marvellously recreated by Robert K. Massie in his book, *Dreadnought*.

King Edward, wearing his uniform of Admiral of the Fleet with its cocked hat and his blue ribbon of the Order of the Garter, left the yacht

The construction of HMS *Dreadnought* in the Royal Dockyard at Portsmouth. *(Courtesy of Imperial War Museum)*

The completed HMS *Dreadnought*, which made all other battleships obsolete. *(Courtesy of Imperial War Museum)*

at eleven-fifteen a.m. and boarded his train for the short trip through the yard. The death of his father-in-law had curtailed some of the planned display, but the King's train nevertheless passed between solid lines of sailors and marines along a route which included four triumphal arches draped with naval flags and scarlet bunting. At eleven-thirty the train arrived beneath the wooden platform and the King climbed stairs lined with red and white satin to find himself in an enclosure surrounded by admirals, government officials, a naval choir, members of the press, and all the foreign naval attachés, senior among them Rear Admiral Carl Coeper of the Imperial German Navy. Over their heads loomed the bow of the *Dreadnought*, garlanded with red and white geraniums.

Fisher was irrepressible. Standing next to the King, he was seen continuously gesturing and describing features of the ship. The Bishop of Winchester began the service with the 107th Psalm: 'They that go down to the sea in ships, that do business in great waters; these see the works of the Lord and his wonder, in the deep,' and ended it by raising his hand to bless the ship and all who would sail in her. When the last blocks had been knocked away and the *Dreadnought* was held only by a single, symbolic cable, the King plucked a bottle of Australian wine from a nest of flowers before him and swung it against the bow. The bottle bounced back. Again his Majesty swung and this time the bottle shattered and wine splashed down the steel plates. 'I christen you *Dreadnought!*' cried the King. Then, taking a chisel and a wooden mallet made from the timbers of Nelson's *Victory*, he went to work on the symbolic rope holding the ship in place. This time, one stroke did the job. The great ship stirred. Slowly at first, then with increasing momentum, she glided backwards down the greased building way. A few minutes later the giant hull floated serenely on the water, corralled by a flotilla of paddle tugs. The band played 'God Save the King,' the crowd gave three cheers, and His Majesty descended the steps.[4]

If young Leach did not read the newspaper accounts of HMS *Dreadnought*'s launching, he certainly heard about it from his father. The reaction of an eleven-year-old English boy to such an event can be fairly guessed. He would have taken enormous pride in the Royal Navy and his country. The long range effect of this event on Jack Leach's life is less easily gauged. Perhaps, at the very least the introduction of a new class of battleship into the Royal Navy, which ensured that Great Britain would retain her naval supremacy, was a factor in Jack Leach's decision to enter the Royal Naval College, Osborne, at an early age.

CHAPTER II

OSBORNE, DARTMOUTH AND THE BATTLE OF JUTLAND

Jack Leach commenced his naval career at the Royal Naval College, Osborne. He was then only thirteen. The transition from family life at Clevedon to the life of a naval cadet at Osborne could not have been easy. Parental visits were not encouraged and he seldom if ever saw them during his time at the college.

Osborne, located on the Isle of Wight, had been a favourite home of Queen Victoria, second only to Balmoral. It was at Osborne that the Queen died on 22 January 1901. She had hoped that her eldest son would make Osborne his official residence; he chose to give the whole of the Osborne Estate to the nation while retaining considerable control over its use. In 1902 or early 1903 'that erratic naval genius, Admiral Sir John Fisher, then Second Sea Lord and in charge of personnel … suggested to King Edward that use might be made of portions of the Osborne Estate for a junior Naval College.'[5] Fisher quickly won King Edward VII's approval. Construction and conversion work commenced in March 1903. On 4 August of the same year the buildings were formally opened by the King accompanied by the Prince of Wales. It is interesting to note that there are striking parallels in the careers of Captain Leach and Admiral of the Fleet Lord Fisher, better known to the lower deck as Jackie Fisher. At only 40 Fisher was appointed Captain of the newest and most power-ful vessel in the Royal Navy, HMS *Inflexible*; at 46 Leach was appointed

John 'Jackie' Fisher, later First Sea Lord as a Rear Admiral in the early 1890s. *(Courtesy of Fisher Family Archives)*

Captain of HMS *Prince of Wales*, then also the newest and most powerful battleship. At 45 Fisher had become Director of Naval Ordnance; at the same age Leach received the appointment. Later the redoubtable Fisher would be twice appointed First Sea Lord. Certainly Leach would never have compared himself to Fisher; yet in early 1941 Leach had achieved an ascendancy that bode well for the future. He was by nature unassuming, but amongst his contemporaries there were more than a few who were sure that his promotion to Flag Rank was only a matter of time.

Cadet John C. Leach entered the Royal Naval College in 1907 as a member of the Exmouth Term. He came into contact with Prince Edward, later King Edward VIII, who was a fellow member of the Exmouth Term. Edward's younger brother, Prince Albert, would enter Osborne two years later. Almost exactly eighteen years after Prince Albert entered Osborne he would spend over four months in the battle-cruiser HMS *Renown* on a round the world voyage, the highlight of which was a Royal Tour of Australia. On that voyage his naval liaison officer was Lieutenant Commander John C. Leach.

Cadet Leach was under a commanding officer who was responsible for discipline and naval instruction and a headmaster who was responsible for his academic studies. These two gentlemen, important though they were, did not have the same degree of influence on his life as the Term Officer. There were only six term officers picked from the wardrooms of the entire Navy. They were senior lieutenants of about 26 or 27. It has been said of them that they moulded the character of the cadets in their charge. Amongst their other duties they organised games and dealt out punishments. Such was the awe in which they were held by the cadets that they were considered demi-gods. Leach was also assigned a tutor who kept close track of his academic progress.

Cadet Leach's two years at Osborne passed with good progress in both his naval instruction and his academic studies. When he left Osborne, he was well prepared for Dartmouth. Dartmouth, the full name of which is the Britannia Royal Naval College, is situated north of the town of Dartmouth on the side of a steep hill where it commands a magnificent view of the River Dart before it reaches the sea. The principal structure, designed by a distinguished architect, Sir Aston Webb, has been called 'a masterpiece of Edwardian Architecture'.[6] Dartmouth, which had been founded two years after Osborne, was a much more serious college and for good reason. In less than three years the cadets at Dartmouth would become midshipmen who would serve in ships of the Royal Navy in all of the exigencies of war. Naval Cadet John C. Leach now wore the regulation full-length naval overcoat instead of the short reefer jacket that he had worn at Osborne. He became conscientious in his dress and wore his uniforms with pride in himself and in the hallowed traditions of a navy that was second to none.

There is a total lack of archival documents about Cadet Leach's career at Osborne; however, there is solid documentation about his career at Dartmouth. While it does not provide a comprehensive record of his life at the college, there are clear indications of his progress as a cadet and prowess on the athletic field. The Summer 1909 issue of *Britannia Magazine* published the term order of merit for the Exmouth Term. Leach was 28th out of a class of 61. He was well ahead of Prince Edward of Wales who was 49th. It was, however, on the playing fields of Dartmouth that he truly excelled.

The same issue of *Britannia Magazine* contains a photograph of Dartmouth's First Eleven. J.C. Leach is standing in the second row. He is wearing white flannel trousers, white boots, a dark single breasted jacket and his college scarf. Leach was approaching his fifteenth birthday, although he looked younger. The magazine also contains a full account of a cricket match in which Leach participated as a bowler. The heading reads 'Britannia RN College (cadets) v. Exeter School.' In addition to Leach the following individuals are mentioned:

Harries, the Captain for Dartmouth and a fieldsman
Bulleid, a batsman for Exeter
Stanton, a bowler for Dartmouth
Twysden, a bowler and fieldsman for Dartmouth
Brown, a bowler for Dartmouth
Clow, a batsman for Exeter

The account of this match begins with a statement of victory. 'This match was played on our ground on Saturday, July 3rd and resulted in a very easy win for us by seven wickets.'[7] The writer continues:

Leach started from the stables end, and off his first ball Harries might have caught Bulleid in the deep field, but he misjudged the catch. ... With the score at 50, Harries changed the bowling (this might, with effect, have been done before), Stanton and Twysden taking the place of Brown and Leach. ... Then Leach, who had gone on again just before, took all before him, another excellent though rather lucky catch by Twysden at mid-on getting rid of Clow. ... After the second wicket fell, our fielding was excellent, but it is a bad sign for fielding to get slack when wickets are not falling. Leach took six for 90, Brown three for 60, and Stanton one for 15.[8]

Leach did not bat.

The Summer 1910 issue of *Britannia Magazine* contains a personal description of the better members of Dartmouth's cricket team. The heading reads, 'First Eleven Characters.'[9]

Leach ... Has bowled admirably throughout the season. Bowls fewer loose balls than formerly, and has developed a good though obvious off-break. Is a poor and timid field. As a bat has few strokes, but can be relied upon to keep his end up.[10]

There is no record of how 15-year-old Leach reacted to the assertion that he was 'a poor and timid field', but one can well imagine.

Leach's 'passing out' from Dartmouth was in April 1911. Earlier that year he had shown much promise in the game of racquets. In the open singles he won four straight games before losing a hard-fought game to Lindsell in the finals 15–4, 8–15, 15–10, 15–6. Then he and Lindsell teamed up in the handicap doubles to win three straight games before winning the finals 15–8, 18–13, 18–13.

Dr Jane E. Harrold, Archivist and Deputy Curator of Britannia Museum, Britannia Royal Naval College, has kindly verified that 'J.C. Leach joined Dartmouth from Osborne, in May 1909, passing out in April 1911. He was a member of the Exmouth Term together with HRH the Prince of Wales.'[11] Dr Harrold is the co-author of the admirable book, *Britannia Royal Naval College 1905–2005, A Century of Officer Training at Dartmouth*. She and Dr Richard Porter have given their readers a vivid description of what Cadet Leach, age sixteen, experienced on the day he passed out:

> The culmination of the young officers' training at Dartmouth is the Passing Out Parade. Traditionally these were held three times a year at the end of each term. The 'Passers Out' would be inspected on the parade ground, followed by a slow march up the steps and into the front door of the College. The door would be slammed shut, and the young officers who have passed out toss their caps into the air to a resounding cheer.[12]

Before he was entitled to wear the dirk and patches of a midshipman, Leach was required to spend up to six months in a cadet training ship. There he learned the practical aspects of seamanship and the basic duties of junior officers in ships of the Royal Navy. His training ship was the 9800-ton armoured cruiser HMS *Cumberland* whose most conspicuous features were her three very tall funnels. This would not be the last time that Leach served in a ship named *Cumberland*. The next time he would be her Captain.

By 1911 the sands of peacetime were rapidly running out. It is not easy to pinpoint the start of the naval race between Britain and Germany, but it was evident on 3 January 1909. On that day Reginald McKenna, the First Lord of the Admiralty, who had become gravely alarmed at German progress in battleship construction, wrote to Prime Minister Asquith:

My dear Prime Minister:

… It seemed to me that an examination of the German Naval Estimates might prove helpful in showing how far Germany is acting secretly and in apparent breach of her law. … I am anxious to avoid alarmist language but I cannot resist the following conclusions which it is my duty to submit to you:

1) Germany is anticipating the shipbuilding programme laid down by the law of 1907.
2) She is doing so secretly.
3) She will certainly have 13 big ships in commission in the spring of 1911.
4) She will probably have 21 big ships in commission in the spring of 1912.
5) German capacity to build dreadnaughts is at this moment equal to ours.

The last conclusion is the most alarming, and if justified would give the public a rude awakening should it become known.[13]

After a furious debate in Parliament a censure motion of Balfour was defeated 353 to 135. This authorised the Admiralty to lay down the keels for eight new battleships instead of the four that had been previously considered. The naval arms race with Germany was well underway.

On 27 September 1911, Prime Minister Asquith was staying at a house provided by one of his brothers-in-law on the coast of East Lothian in Scotland, 'a restful place, with an avenue of lime trees, an exceptional library, and a private golf course stretching down to the sea.'[14] His house guest was the Home Secretary, 36-year-old Winston Churchill. That afternoon they played golf. The Prime Minister's daughter, Violet Asquith, recalled an encounter with Winston following their game: 'I was just finishing tea when they came in. Looking up, I saw in Winston's face a radiance like the sun.' She asked whether he would like tea. He looked at her 'with grave but shining eyes. "No, I don't want tea. I don't want anything, anything in the world. Your father has just offered me the Admiralty."'[15]

Churchill did not believe that a war with Germany was inevitable, but he did believe that British naval supremacy was essential. In February 1912 in Glasgow Churchill gave a major address that provoked both the Germans and the pacifist wing of the Liberal Party.

> The British Navy is to us a necessity and … the German Navy is to them more in the nature of a luxury. Our naval power involves British exist-ence. It is existence to us; it is expansion to them. We cannot menace the peace of a single continental hamlet, no matter how great and supreme our Navy may become. But, on the other hand, the whole fortunes of our race and Empire, the whole treasure accumulated during so many centu-ries of sacrifice and achievement would perish and be swept utterly away if our naval supremacy were to be impaired. It is the British Navy which makes Great Britain a great power. But Germany was a great power, respected and honoured all over the world, before she had a single ship.[16]

At the stroke of midnight on 4 August 1914, Great Britain declared war on Germany when Britain's ultimatum demanding that Germany with-draw her Army from Belgium expired. John Catterall Leach was 27 days from his twentieth birthday. He was no longer a midshipman. He now wore the stripe of a sub-lieutenant of the Royal Navy. In less than two years he was promoted to Lieutenant. His most important sea duty during the First World War was in the battleship HMS *Erin*. *Erin* was a new battleship with a curious past; she had been built by the British shipbuilder Vickers for the Turkish Navy. Her ordnance was formidable. She mounted ten 13.5-inch guns in five turrets and sixteen 6-inch guns in individual barbettes. She was also armed with four submerged tor-pedo tubes. With a length of 559 feet 9 inches, a beam of 91 feet 7 inches and a standard displacement of 22,780 tons she was smaller than the Queen Elizabeth class of British battleships, which were the best the Royal Navy had in 1914. Churchill, as First Lord of the Admiralty, sum-marily requisitioned *Erin* as she was nearing completion. The Turkish government considered his action manifestly illegal. Churchill's action proved prescient as Turkey soon entered the war on Germany's side.

Lieutenant Leach's first experience with a fleet engagement came on 29 May 1916 at the Battle of Jutland, known in Germany as the Battle of the Skagerrak. It was the largest naval battle in history and involved vir-tually every battleship and battle cruiser in both navies. The greater part

Winston Churchill as First
Lord of the Admiralty.
*(Courtesy of Imperial War
Museum)*

of the British Fleet was at Scapa Flow under the command of Admiral
Sir John Jellicoe. The lesser part consisting of six battle cruisers and one
squadron of four fast and powerful Queen Elizabeth class battleships was
at Rosyth under the command of Vice Admiral Sir David Beatty.

HMS *Erin* was part of Admiral Jellicoe's main battle fleet of 28 battleships. In the initial encounter the impetuous Beatty led his battle
cruisers in a cavalry-like charge at the five battle cruisers of Admiral
Hipper's Scouting Group One. It proved disastrous for the Royal Navy.
Two of Beatty's lightly armoured cruisers were blown up while Hipper
lost none. Belatedly, Beatty ordered a withdrawal to the north in order
to lure the entire German Fleet into an engagement with Jellicoe's
vastly superior force. At 18.01 on 31 May HMS *Lion*, Beatty's flagship,
came within sight of Jellicoe who signalled, 'Where is the enemy's battle
fleet?'[17] The answer was ambiguous, but it was clear to Jellicoe that
action was imminent and he ordered his six columns of battleships into
line. The German vessels soon came within sight. By the classic tactic of

crossing the 'T' of the German line the British battleships were able to fire broadsides into the German ships which could only reply with their forward turrets.

Erin, which was positioned toward the end of the line of Jellicoe's battleships, was never able to bring her main armament to bear on the enemy. The Captain of *Erin*, the Honourable V.A. Stanley MVO, had been the commanding officer of Britannia Royal Naval College. On the first day of the war, it was he who had received the famous Admiralty telegram that simply said, 'Mobilise'.

Three and a half months after the Battle of Jutland Lieutenant Leach was mentioned in dispatches. A supplement to the *London Gazette*, no 29751, published by authority of the Admiralty on 15 September 1916 read, 'Performed very good service as officer in charge of a turret.'[18] The same issue announced that the seniority of Acting Lieutenant John Catterall Leach is to be antedated to 30 June 1916. Both before and after the Battle of Jutland Captain Stanley gave Leach exemplary fitness reports. On 16 May he wrote, 'Cannot speak too highly of him. His work is always of a high standard.'[19] Then on 17 June he wrote, 'Very reliable and thoroughly trustworthy; of marked ability.'[20]

In numerical terms the Battle of Jutland was a German victory as the British suffered far greater losses than they inflicted. The battle cruisers *Indefatigable*, *Invincible* and *Queen Mary* had been sunk as were three armoured cruisers and eight destroyers. A total of 6,097 British sailors perished. The Germans had lost the battle cruiser *Lützow*, a pre-Dreadnought battleship, four light cruisers and five torpedo boats; 2,551 German sailors died.

While three of the fast British battleships, *Warspite*, *Barham* and *Malaya* had suffered extensive damage requiring dockyard repairs, the main battle fleet, including *Erin*, was unscathed. The Grand Fleet still out-numbered the German Fleet by 28 Dreadnoughts to 16. The military historian John Keegan noted that

For more than half the war, therefore – from 1 June 1916 until 11 November 1918, 29 months in all – the High Seas Fleet was at best 'a fleet in being', and for its last year scarcely even that ... the central factor in the reduction of the High Seas Fleet to an inoperative force was the action of Jutland itself.'[21]

In strategic terms Jutland was undoubtedly a British victory. Jutland dominated British naval thinking for over two decades. For many it confirmed that the battleship was the 'Queen of Battle'. For many it established that, for the indefinite future, the fleet having the largest number of battleships with the heaviest guns and the thickest armour would always prevail. Jutland emphasised the importance of the gunnery officer. Afterwards the best and brightest young officers in the Royal Navy gravitated toward gunnery. Lieutenant J.C. Leach was already a gunnery officer but Jutland may have influenced his decision to make gunnery his speciality for the rest of his career.

That summer Leach had more than just Jutland on his mind. He had fallen in love with Miss Evelyn Burrell Lee of Bovey Tracey, Devon. He was determined to win her heart and to gain her father's approval of their marriage. He succeeded on both counts.

CHAPTER III

EVELYN BURRELL LEACH

On 9 September 1916 at Bovey Tracey in Devon, Lieutenant John C. Leach married Miss Evelyn Burrell Lee, the only daughter of Richard Henry Lee, master of Yarner, his nearby magical country estate. When they commenced their life together, the end of the First World War was still over two years away. At the beginning and at the end, their marriage would be under the clouds of war. Notwithstanding two world wars separated by a tenuous peace, their marriage would be a joy to both of them, to their two sons and to everyone who knew them.

Lieutenant Leach had clearly given some thought to his choice of best man at his wedding. His first choice could not, however, accept the honour because he was at sea. His second choice was rather a surprise, a French teacher at Dartmouth called Percy Bashford. Subsequently, Bashford never had a significant place in Leach's life but went on to marry the widow of Sir Arthur Sullivan, who with Sir William Gilbert established the distinctive English form of the operetta including *HMS Pinafore* and *The Pirates of Penzance*.

In the midst of a war which allowed only a brief leave of absence, the young couple's decision to have a small wedding was almost made for them. Had they married in peacetime, quite a few of Leach's Royal Navy friends would have been present. In the event Lieutenant Leach's fellow officers from the gun room of HMS *Erin* presented the bride and groom with a gift that they would cherish for the rest of their lives, a silver salver.

The link between this silver salver and the Royal Navy continues to the present day. Through the generosity of Admiral of the Fleet Sir Henry Leach and his late wife, Mary, it has been made into the 'HMS *Nottingham* Man of the Year Plate.' *Nottingham* is a Type 42 destroyer. Each year this plate is awarded to the member of the ship's company who in the previous twelve months has consistently performed beyond the call of duty.

The home that Richard H. Lee purchased just before the Great War

> ... is a Grade II listed seventeenth-century building but its origins are much older. *The Devon Place Names* book gives the place name Yarner as deriving from the old English [i.e. Anglo Saxon] for eagle bank or slope. It appears in the Patent Rolls of 1344 as Yarnuor/Yarnouere and in the Court Rolls of 1399 as Yarner.[22]

When Lieutenant Leach and his bride first made Yarner their home it consisted of 4 acres of gardens, 60 acres of farmland, and 800 acres of wood. The structures included the main house with walls four feet thick in places, 'priest holes' half way up the chimneys, battlements near the roof line and a slate roof. Behind the house were a large stable area and a coach house leading to farm buildings and a large garage.

In future years Evelyn and John would create their favourite garden, a water garden. The house, which had been built halfway up a steep hill, faced northeast. Even in the summer it never got full sun and was, therefore, deliciously cool. They had a magnificent view to the northeast toward Exeter and from the moor above their home they had an equally splendid view to the southeast toward Torquay.

There is a fine description of Yarner written after John and Evelyn's children were born.

> The outdoor staff included a cowman, woodman, chauffeur, gamekeeper and gardeners. The chauffeur, Jack Shepherd, married a local girl and lived at Pottery Road. He is particularly remembered for keeping the cars immaculate and taking the boys of the family fishing ... Another character from the outside staff was Mr Heathman, the head gardener. Described as a quiet man who wore glasses, he had a glass eye that constantly

dropped out, necessitating a search amongst the plants. Consequently his colleagues called him Winkie … Mr and Mrs Lee's daughter, Evelyn, married Captain John Catterall Leach RN. When Mr Lee died Mrs Leach and her mother stayed on, with Mrs Lee having responsibility for the house and Evelyn Leach for the garden, which was her pride and joy. The acid soil of the garden encouraged rhododendrons, azaleas, magnolia and primulas. There was also a rose garden and herbaceous borders. The rock and water gardens were of local granite and the huge specimen trees were a feature, including a copper beech by the rock garden and a Scots pine in the centre of the lawn. In the kitchen garden was a mix of soft fruit and vegetables. Around the walls were apple trees.[23]

Yarner offered superb opportunities for fly fishing that John had seldom enjoyed before. It encompassed a mile-and-a-half of river front along the Bovey where he could fish for trout. John was also attracted by the gardens. In time he would become a keen gardener.

In the early years of their marriage the couple lost a child in infancy. They were then blessed with two healthy baby boys, Roger Lee Leach, born 10 December 1919, and Henry Leach, born 18 November 1923. They lost another baby only a few years later. For both boys Yarner was an extremely happy home, yet it must be said that after losing her first child, Evelyn was inclined to be overly protective toward her next child, Roger. For John and Evelyn, Yarner would be their only home during their 25 years of marriage.

From 1923 to 1925 Leach was mostly absent from home. He was then a full lieutenant and the fleet gunnery officer in HMS *Calcutta*, a light cruiser later converted into an anti-aircraft ship. She was the flagship of the America and West Indies Station and her home port was Bermuda. This gave rise to a grand adventure for the whole Leach family when they all moved to Bermuda. No cars were allowed on the island and the summer temperatures discouraged them from taking long walks. In order to provide transportation for his family Lieutenant Leach arranged for a carriage and team of horses to be shipped out from Yarner. Apparently the horses did not mind the heat. Shortly after the Leach family returned to Yarner, Andrew Browne Cunningham, later Admiral of the Fleet Viscount Cunningham of Hyndhope, became Captain of the *Calcutta*. In May 1926 he took the re-commissioned ship and new ship's company to Bermuda. He has left a candid picture of the social life of Bermuda, which the Leach family had experienced only a few months earlier.

> On arriving at Bermuda we berthed inside the dockyard. I reported myself to the Commander-in-Chief, Vice Admiral Sir James Fergusson, and made the acquaintance of his wife and four daughters ... The weeks passed pleasantly enough with dinner parties at Admiralty House and Government House, but most pleasantly of all were the supper parties in the grounds of Admiralty House with Lady Fergusson and her daughters, while the Admiral had a stag party. We used to spread out our meal near the gravestone of one Francis, a midshipman, whom rumour said had been knifed by the Admiralty House butler in the early nineteenth century for undue familiarity with a housemaid.[24]

There would be only two other occasions when Evelyn joined her husband in a foreign duty station. In 1933 or 1934 she went out to be with her husband in Malta, which was the home port of the Mediterranean Fleet. Malta was even hotter year round than Bermuda. In the mid 1930s she spent a year in the Far East (together with Roger) in order to be near her husband, who then commanded the heavy cruiser HMS *Cumberland* on the China Station. She and her son resided in the British community of Wei-Hai-Wei, a delectable little island on the north side of the Shantung Promontory. With its fine natural harbour it had been an important British naval base for over 30 years. In 1930 the British voluntarily surrendered their lease, but the Royal Navy continued to make it a port of call until late in 1938 when it was seized by the Japanese. After 1930 Wei-Hai-Wei retained its British colonial atmosphere with a club, a hospital and comfortable living quarters.

Wherever she was Evelyn found the social aspects of Navy life pleasant and rewarding; however, she was never content with an endless round of cocktail parties. She devoted much time and effort in helping the wives of junior officers who were experiencing difficulties, frequently visiting those who were confined to hospital, actions which won her the love and respect of her contemporaries. At home with the boys she was a strict but scrupulously fair disciplinarian. Her younger son recalls that 'if Mummy says it is, it is, even if it isn't.'

Before the outbreak of the Second World War the family would take their summer holiday at a tiny seaside resort on the north coast of

Cornwall called Polzeath. Roger and Henry were then old enough to amuse themselves; their mother may have been a bit lonely. Most summers her husband was only able to join them for the odd weekend. Evelyn knew how much her husband loved to take their boys fishing and she greatly encouraged these all too infrequent outings. Their favourite river was the nearby Dart. The threesome would leave Yarner in the late afternoon and often enjoyed 'the Spitchwick Water' of a late summer evening. Starting about 18.00 they would fish (never with success when it came to salmon) for a couple of hours. Then they would wait for darkness during which time they had a picnic supper. When the bats came out and they could no longer see their flies, they took up their prime positions on Webburn Pool where the River Webburn, a tributary, runs into the Dart. There they would fish for sea trout, known to the locals as Peal, using 9-foot rods and light tackle. Around 23.00 the fish seemed to go to bed and the three of them would then head back to Yarner, tired but happy. Once young Henry landed a beautiful 5-pounder, a thrill he still remembers.

Evelyn Burrell Lee Leach was a lady of substance who played a vital role in her husband's life and in the lives of her two boys, the younger of whom has written of his mother:

> I was blessed with exceptional parents to whom I was devoted – more so than I realised at the age of ten. They had married young and there could not have been a more devoted couple; twenty years later they might have been thought to be on their honeymoon. Home [Yarner] on the edge of Dartmoor near the village of Bovey Tracey, was a very happy place.
>
> Mother was beautiful with raven black hair, a lovely neck and clear grey eyes set in a rounded face above a humorous mouth. She was highly intelligent, soft-spoken and very strict, but always scrupulously fair, so that I knew exactly where I stood; a brilliant organiser, resolutely determined and with a bubbling sense of humour and appreciation of the ridiculous. She herself had a strong streak of naughtiness and was always game for a bit of fun. She had the guts of ten and little would stop her in the particular pursuit of the moment – especially if she knew she was right (as she normally thought she was!).[25]

The life of the wife of a Royal Navy officer has never been easy. For Evelyn her husband's naval career meant long separations when he was at sea, modest pay for most of his career, infrequent wartime leaves, and finally, tragedy. Yet, there was never a time when she asked him to resign the King's Commission and take up a new vocation that would involve fewer separations and less danger. Throughout their marriage she was a valiant companion.

Chapter IV

Between the Wars

Fewer than four years after the German sailors had scuttled the High Seas Fleet at Scapa Flow, the Admiralty was faced with another fleet that was a potential threat to the British Empire. This foe emerged almost overnight in 1922 when Britain allowed the Anglo-Japanese Alliance of 1902 to lapse. For twenty years this largely forgotten treaty was the cornerstone of British policy in Asia. In his comprehensive work *A History of the Modern World from 1917 to the 1980s* Paul Johnson considers the ending of this alliance a watershed event.

> And as long as Britain was Japan's ally, the latter had a prime interest in preserving her own internal respectability, constitutional propriety and the rule of law, all of which Britain had taught her. This was why the destruction of the Anglo-Japanese alliance by the USA and Canada in 1921–22 was so fatal to peace in the Far East.[26]

Johnson seems to assume that if this treaty had remained intact, Britain could have gently nudged Japan into a peaceful democracy that posed no threat to her neighbours in the Far East, much less to Britain and the US. Perhaps such a beneficent outcome was possible, perhaps not. Johnson would be the first to concede that the Japanese were not well understood by many in the West. For centuries Japan was known by its people as 'the land of the rising sun', and the Japanese believed in the divinity of their Emperor by virtue of his descent from the sun goddess. It is therefore not surprising that many of the leaders of the Japanese armed forces considered that Japan had a sacred mission to rule all of Asia, including those areas colonised by Britain, France, Holland and the US. The Japanese people, furthermore, were well aware of the vast natural resources, in particular oil, that the 'White Man' controlled. It was not hard for their military leaders to fan the flames of resentment.

Japanese aggression did not commence with the lapse of the Anglo-Japanese Alliance in 1922; it had commenced a quarter of a century earlier in 1894–95 with the conquest of Formosa. In 1904 Japan surprised Russia with a deadly attack on Port Arthur, inflicting a humiliating defeat on its foe during the ensuing war. In 1910 Japan conquered and then annexed the ancient Kingdom of Korea. In 1914 she entered the First World War as an ally of Britain and France, her underlying motivation being the acquisition of Germany's colonies in the Pacific. These included a German naval base in the Shantung Peninsula not far from the British naval base at Hei-Wai-Hei and a vast area in the central and western Pacific encompassing island groups that would become famous battlegrounds in the Second World War. These were the Marianas (except Guam, which the US had purchased in 1899), the Carolines and the Marshalls. Truk in the Carolines would become one of the most important staging areas for the Imperial Japanese Navy.

In the two decades after the lapse of the treaty between Britain and Japan, the latter engaged in even more blatant aggression. In the 1930s Japan sought to conquer China. Japan was now on a collision course with Britain and the US that would eventually involve one of the Royal Navy's newest battleships, HMS *Prince of Wales*.

The potential threat of the Japanese Navy after the Anglo-Japanese Treaty lapsed was hardly a pressing issue for Lieutenant Leach, who had more immediate concerns. Leach served as a Lieutenant from 15 December 1915 to 15 December 1923 before he was promoted to Lieutenant Commander; it was customary to serve as a lieutenant for eight years. During that time he served as the gunnery officer of HMS *Stuart* – a destroyer flotilla leader later sold to the Australian Navy – and as Ship's and Fleet Gunnery Officer in HMS *Calcutta*, a light cruiser, which was destined to be sunk by German aircraft during the evacuation from Crete on 30 May 1941. While in HMS *Calcutta* (1923–

25) his son, Henry, was born at Yarner. On 15 December Leach learned of his promotion to Lieutenant Commander and as previously noted, the family moved to Bermuda.

In September 1925 Leach reported to the Royal Naval Staff College at Greenwich for a staff course that lasted well into the next year. His next sea assignment was as gunnery officer of HMS *Renown*. The *Renown* was a 32,000-ton battle cruiser armed with six 15-inch guns and twenty 4.5-inch dual purpose guns. She was the first ship of the Renown Class of battle cruisers. The only other ship of this class was the ill-fated HMS *Repulse*. *Renown* and *Repulse* were begun on the same day, 25 January 1915.

Being the gunnery officer of a battle cruiser was a new experience for Leach. His previous gunnery experience at sea had been in HMS *Stuart*, whose main armament was 4.7-inch guns, and HMS *Calcutta*, whose main armament was 6-inch guns. The heavy guns of the *Renown* had over twice the range of the latter but a slower rate of fire. Leach mastered his new assignment, having greatly benefited from his gunnery courses – the Long Gunnery Course at Whale Island, the Royal Navy's main gunnery school HMS *Excellent*, and later the Devonport Gunnery School.

In July 1926 when Lieutenant Commander Leach first walked up the gangway and saluted the quarterdeck in HMS *Renown* he had no way of knowing that within six months he would be in close contact with a future sovereign, King George VI. King George V had chosen his second son, the Duke of York, to represent the monarchy at the formal transfer of the Australian Parliament to the new legislative building in the new capital, Canberra. The decision was not an easy one. The King felt that his son lacked confidence and he feared a recurrence of his son's stutter. Fortunately, a few months before his departure for Australia, the Duke of York had been able to overcome his speech impediment through the help of a remarkable specialist called Lionel Logue, who happened to be Australian. Nevertheless, the Duke of York shared his father's misgivings. Whilst he felt it was his duty to go on the royal tour, he knew that he and the Duchess of York would miss their baby daughter, Princess Elizabeth. Furthermore, they would not be with her on her first birthday, 21 April 1927. The prince was faced with an arduous journey involving numerous official appearances and speeches:

Sail from Portsmouth, January 6, 1927 – Las Palmas – Jamaica – Colón – Panama – the Marquesas Islands – Fiji – arrive New Zealand (Auckland), February 22 – leave New Zealand (Kingston), March 22 – arrive Australia (Sydney), March 26 – leave Australia (Perth), May 23 – Mauritius – Port Said – Malta – Gibraltar – return Portsmouth, June 27.[27]

The Royal Tour proved to be a huge success and the Duke experienced no serious recurrence of his stutter. The people of New Zealand and Australia were taken with these two handsome, gracious representatives of the Royal Family. Lieutenant Commander Leach contributed significantly to the tour's success, having had the honour of being the 'ship liaison officer' for the Duke and Duchess. It was a felicitous assignment. The two men were only slightly over a year apart and had both passed out of Osborne and Dartmouth, been present at the Battle of Jutland (though in different ships) and both loved the Royal Navy. They had much in common.

Leach's first glimpse of the Duke of York may well have been when the Prince of Wales bade him farewell on the Portsmouth quayside, an occasion captured in an official photograph. Both future sovereigns are smartly dressed in their dark blue uniforms with swords encased in sheaths on their belts. The Prince of Wales is wearing white gloves and both men have four gold rings on their sleeves. The two books written about the Royal Tour are *The Royal Embassy, The Duke and Duchess of York's Tour in Australasia* by Ian F.M. Lucas and *The Royal Tour of the Duke and Duchess of York* by Taylor Darbyshire. Lucas's book contains what may well be the only photograph taken on the Royal Tour of Leach and the future King of England. The caption reads, 'T.R.H. bid farewell to the officers of *Renown* off Spithead.' The photograph captures a Lieutenant Commander in The Royal Navy gracefully bowing to the Duke of York at the same time that he extends his right hand. The officer is clearly taller than the Duke and has very broad shoulders and a trim, athletic build. The photograph also reveals that he has a prominent nose. These physical characteristics match those of Leach, who was 6′ 2″, had unusually broad shoulders and a rather 'forthright' nose. It is possible that this photograph is of one of the other half a dozen lieutenant commanders in *Renown*'s company, but it seems unlikely.

Darbyshire's book provides a brief, but vivid, description of Leach's dual roles as gunnery officer and liaison officer to the Duke and Duchess of York.

Then there was Lieutenant–Commander J.C. Leach, the popular 'Guns' who had been primarily responsible for the 'shoot' arranged for the benefit of the Dominion Premiers a few months before, when the *Renown*, but fresh from the Dry-dock, had scored a hundred per cent efficiency test, and was specifically congratulated thereon by the Commander-in-Chief of the Battle-Cruiser Squadron when he hauled down his flag. It was 'Guns' who, to his other duties, added that of *liaison* officer between the ship's company and the Royal party. His functions, indeed, were innumerable; not only did he act as a connecting-link between the two, but it was his task to organise the attendance of the officers at all the official and private functions for which invitations had been received – of which more anon.

And the word 'Social' suggests anew one of the most important, as it was one of the most exacting, duties of 'Guns'. It was his task before every port and during every stay in port to see that the invitations, which arrived on board in shoals, were properly accepted. It was a real business, too, for very naturally, everybody was anxious to have as guests the officers of the *Renown*, and there were comparatively few 'to go around'. There must have been hundreds of such invitations to arrange for, and the thorough way it was done by 'Guns' was worthy of all admiration.[28]

On the return voyage to England from the west coast of Australia Captain Sulivan was called upon to deal with an emergency that all captains dread: a fire at sea. On 26 May, over 1,000 miles west of Fremantle, a fire was discovered in 'D' boiler-room, caused by an overflow of fuel oil from one of the tanks. The standard procedure was to cut off all air and let the fire burn itself out, but there was a major complication, a large in-draught fan working on its own steam that had to be turned off manually.

The principal responsibility for containing and extinguishing this fire rested with the Engineer-Commander. Lieutenant Commander Leach was also directly involved; he needed to make certain that the fire did not reach the ship's magazines. To do so he ordered a gunner's mate stationed at each magazine so that he could flood it in case the temperature rose above the danger point. If this fire had spread to other oil tanks, Captain Sulivan would have had to abandon ship. Throughout the crisis there was a complete absence of panic and the fire was finally put out towards midnight.

The remainder of the voyage back to Portsmouth passed serenely except for a few periods of foul weather. There were three memorable evenings on board that brought the Duke of York and Lieutenant Commander Leach together. 31 May was the eleventh anniversary of the Battle of Jutland. Only six members of the wardroom mess had been present at the battle. That night Leach and the other five celebrated the Royal Navy's victory by dining together. Afterwards Captain Sulivan, the Duke and the Duke's naval equerry, Lieutenant Commander Buist, all of whom were at Jutland, joined the party. For the King's son, who felt more at ease with Royal Navy officers than he did with the British aristocracy, this opportunity to share memories of a famous victory with a small gathering of his naval friends was probably one of the highlights of the voyage.

The night after HMS *Renown* departed from Gibraltar, the Duke and Duchess were guests of the wardroom at dinner. In a few well chosen words the Duke paid tribute to the spirit of camaraderie that existed among *Renown*'s officers. He then presented to the Commander as President of the Mess a beautiful silver cup as a small memento of the voyage. After dinner the Duke and Duchess stood around the piano and sang old English and Scottish songs; the Duchess came from the Scottish aristocracy and was very fond of her homeland. Their Royal Highnesses' last night in *Renown* was Sunday, 26 June. They spent their evening in the wardroom. When the time came, they joined hands and sang *Auld Lang Syne*.

In less than ten years the Duke of York would become King George VI. During his reign he would never have meaningful contact with any of the officers from *Renown* except the one known as 'Guns'. Leach and the Duke of York had established a real rapport, and he was also on friendly terms with the future Queen Mother. The best evidence of Leach's contribution to the Royal Tour was the King's decision on the recommendation of the Duke of York to appoint him a Member of the Royal Victorian Order, MVO.

Leach had not neglected his duties as gunnery officer in favour of dining with royalty. At the end of his assignment in HMS *Renown* Leach received the following evaluations by his Captain, S.R. Bailey, and by Vice Admiral F.C. Dreyer:

> Outstanding officer of exceptional merit and professional qualities, has charm of manner, tact and gift of leadership to an unusual degree. A keen

all round sportsman, fine athlete, always fit. Should have fine career before him. Sgd. Capt. S.R. Bailey[29]

Entirely agree. Exceptionally able officer. Sgd.Vice Admiral F.C. Dreyer[30]

On 31 December 1928 Leach was promoted to Commander. Thus, at the age of 34, he was eligible to be the executive officer of any ship in the Royal Navy; as it turned out he was not to receive an assignment at sea for over three years.

On 29 January 1929 he commenced a one-year stint at the Army Staff College at Camberley in Surrey. The college had been established in 1858 to enable mid-career Army officers to enhance their professional skills. For the Admiralty to send a brand-new commander there seems extraordinary unless the Admiralty foresaw that at some future point Leach would be involved in operations with the Army. In any event the Army General who evaluated Leach's year at Camberley wrote:

Strong character with tact and firmness. Has VG grasp of army matters. Keen, intelligent and has sound judgment. An exceptional officer
on standard of fellow students. Invaluable in problems of combined
operations.
Sgd. Major General C.W. Gynn[31]

The report is dated 30 November 1929. Apparently Commander Leach was able to enjoy an extended leave because his next assignment, directing staff at the Naval Staff College Greenwich, did not commence until 14 April 1930.

On 8 May 1932 Commander Leach became the executive officer of HMS *Royal Oak*, a 21,150-ton battleship with a main armament of eight 15-inch guns. At the outset of the Second World War she was one of the Royal Navy's older battleships having been launched in 1914. She was also another of the Royal Navy's ill fated vessels. In the early hours of 14 October 1939 U-boat captain Günther Prien managed to slip into Scapa Flow and sink *Royal Oak* with three well placed torpedoes before making good his escape.

In 1932 *Royal Oak* was deployed in the Mediterranean Fleet. In those years the Admiralty could take comfort in good relations with France and Italy whose fleets and air forces lay athwart the principal line of communication between Britain and Suez and everything east of the latter. The remainder of the 1930s brought Leach both a coveted promotion and highly important assignments. On 31 December 1933 he was promoted to captain. His career in the Royal Navy was advancing ahead of most of his Dartmouth term mates. On 7 March 1934, Captain Leach took up an appointment in the Admiralty for the first time in his naval career, becoming Deputy Director of Training with other staff duties. While this assignment might not have given him the same satisfaction as being the captain of his own ship, Leach performed his new duties very well indeed, as revealed by the evaluations of two of his senior officers dated 7 March 1936.

> An officer of outstanding ability and personality. A fine type of naval officer. The above remarks embrace all the characteristics mentioned in Section IV of instructions which are possessed by this officer to an exceptional degree.
> Sgd. Captain F.A. Buckley[32]

> Concur. This officer should go far; a fine character and most able.
> Sgd. Rear Admiral C.E .Kennedy-Purvis[33]

Of all the high-ranking officers in the Royal Navy who evaluated Captain Leach, Admiral Kennedy-Purvis was one of the best. Kennedy-Purvis later became Deputy First Sea Lord, of whom Admiral of the Fleet Viscount Cunningham later wrote:

> I found a strong team on the naval side at the Admiralty, and several old friends. The Deputy First Sea Lord was Admiral Sir Charles Kennedy-Purvis, whose wise mind, great ability and knowledge of Admiralty departments and methods were invaluable in relieving the First Sea Lord of much of the administrative work.[34]

On 4 May 1936 Captain John C. Leach took command of HMS *Cumberland*, a 9,750-ton heavy cruiser completed in 1928. She was originally armed with 8 8-inch guns, 8 4-inch anti-aircraft guns and 20 smaller anti-aircraft guns. Before Leach assumed command, *Cumberland* had undergone a major refit, which took over a year. Main alterations included a large hangar and additional aircraft, increased armour protection and improved anti-aircraft armament. Two 4-inch anti-aircraft guns were replaced by four 4-inch MK XVII guns on twin mountings. She was, therefore, a much more modern ship than Leach's last cruiser, *Calcutta*, which had been completed in 1919. HMS *Cumberland* was Captain Leach's first sea command and she would become his favourite ship. However, being captain had its drawbacks. Leach enjoyed the companionship of his fellow officers but when *Cumberland* was at sea he would no longer be able to dine in the wardroom with them. *Cumberland* was the flagship of the China Station and Leach was fortunate to be Flag Captain to two admirals whom he liked and respected, the first being Admiral Sir Charles Little and the second, Admiral Sir Percy Noble.

Leach's first year as captain of HMS *Cumberland* was somewhat uneventful except for one of the most momentous events in the history of the British monarchy. At 10.00 on Thursday 10 December 1936, in England at a place called Fort Belvedere, in the presence of his three younger brothers, King Edward VIII did what no other King of England had ever done; he voluntarily relinquished the throne by signing an instrument of abdication. He took this momentous step in order to marry the American divorcée Wallis Simpson, an event which shocked and dismayed the British public. The shock waves reached HMS *Cumberland* in Hong Kong harbour. Captain Leach's personal views about the abdication are unknown, but there can be little doubt about his favourable opinion of the successor to the throne. On 12 December, under the direction of her Captain, *Cumberland*'s company gave three cheers for the new King and on the same day *Cumberland*'s guard and band paraded in Hong Kong' Queen Square in honour of King George VI. On Sunday 13 December, the customary divine service took place on the quarterdeck of *Cumberland*. The chaplain's prayer, which began with the words 'for our most gracious King George VI' was identical to the prayers said throughout the Churches and Cathedrals of Britain. *Cumberland*'s Captain and many of her officers and ratings silently prayed for this resolute, yet diffident, Royal Navy officer who had never wanted to be King.

The year 1937 proved eventful. The Sino-Japanese War had commenced in September 1931, resulting in the occupation of Manchuria and the creation of the puppet state of Manchukuo. The conflict then took on a new and dangerous dimension in July 1937. The American naval historian Samuel Eliot Morison described the opening of hostilities: 'When the Army was ready, it invaded China proper. That was the famous "China Incident" of 7 July 1937, a cooked-up clash between Japanese troops on manoeuvres and a Chinese outpost on the Marco Polo Bridge near Peiping.'[35] Before the year was out the Japanese Army had committed horrific atrocities in their infamous 'Rape of Nanking'.

The American naval presence in the Far East in August 1937 consisted of the Yangtze River gun-boat flotilla of which the *Panay* was one, a flotilla of destroyers based at the north China port of Chefao, a dozen submarines, a few auxiliaries and a heavy cruiser, USS *Augusta*. On 14 August 1937 *Augusta*, the flagship of the United States Asiatic Fleet, was moored to a buoy near HMS *Cumberland* on the Whangpoo River. That day the *Augusta* was subjected to a bombing attack by the Chinese rather than the Japanese. Captain Leach witnessed at least one bomb explode off the starboard quarter deck of the *Augusta*, the Chinese pilot having apparently mistaken her for a Japanese cruiser. Fortunately, the American ship was undamaged.

On 28 August the British ambassador to China, Sir Hughe Knatchbull-Hugessen, was travelling in a two-car procession from Nanking to Shanghai. The Union Jack was mounted on the right front wing of his Rolls-Royce. Without warning Japanese aircraft strafed the defenceless vehicles, seriously wounding the ambassador. The foreign secretary, Anthony Eden, demanded a formal apology, punishment of those responsible and action by the Japanese authorities to prevent any recurrence of similar incidents. Later Eden would write, 'after further pressure from London, the Japanese government conveyed a formal and public expression of their deep regret and a less satisfactory assurance about the punishment of those responsible.'[36]

On 12 December Japanese naval aircraft committed another outrageous act. On that day USS *Panay* was proceeding upriver on the Yangtze from Nanking with evacuees from the American Embassy while at the same time escorting three Standard Oil barges that sought a safe haven from the Japanese Army. *Panay* was a shoal-draft gunboat with a displacement of 450 tons and a cruising speed of 14 knots. Her main armament were two 3-inch 50 calibre guns. Her anti-aircraft armament consisted of ten light machine guns. That day *Panay* was under the command of Lieutenant Commander J.J. Hughes. The American flag had been hoisted on her mast and was also painted on her awning and topside. Without warning *Panay* was attacked by 24 Japanese naval aircraft that included 15 dive bombers and 9 fighters. *Panay* fought back with her machine guns, but it was clear from the outset that she never had a chance. The first bombs disabled the *Panay*'s forward 3-inch gun, wrecked the wheelhouse, sick bay and fire room and wounded Captain Hughes. After 35 minutes of bombing and strafing with *Panay*'s main deck awash, Hughes ordered the crew to abandon ship. Out of a company of 65, plus an unknown number of civilians, two sailors and one civilian passenger were killed; eleven officers and men were seriously wounded. Two of the three large oil barges were destroyed. It was an act of war.

On the same day the Royal Navy also had gun boats proceeding upriver on the Yangtze. One of them was HMS *Ladybird*. She was larger and better armed than the *Panay*, with a displacement of 625 tons and a speed of 14 knots. She was armed with two 6-inch guns, one 3-inch anti-aircraft gun and 10 smaller anti-aircraft guns. When *Ladybird* was some distance downstream from *Panay*, she was suddenly engaged by Japanese shore batteries, which managed to hit her four times, killing a rating and seriously wounding another. Later that day Japanese aircraft dropped bombs on a concentration of British merchant ships in the Yangtze near Nanking and on the British gunboats *Scarab* and *Cricket* guarding them.

Cumberland under command of Captain Leach was then near Hong Kong far to the south. However, he was soon notified of the attacks on the *Panay* and the *Ladybird*. If these unprovoked Japanese attacks had led to war, *Cumberland*'s situation would have been perilous. Heavy units of the Japanese Navy could have overwhelmed her long before reinforcements reached the China Station.

In the last five months of 1937 HMS *Cumberland* and USS *Augusta* were in frequent contact. It is likely that Admiral Little and Captain Leach held long discussions with their American counterparts about the possibility of war with Japan. Leach would not see *Augusta* again for several years; when he did, he had occasion to focus his telescope on her bridge. There a man wearing a light suit was talking to *Augusta*'s captain. Churchill would later refer to him as 'the greatest American friend we have ever known.'[37] The place was Placentia Bay in Newfoundland, and the man in the light suit was President Franklin D. Roosevelt.

In December and January, Prime Minister Chamberlain followed events in the Far East with a certain amount of disdain for the Japanese.

One year hence, in September 1938, Chamberlain was willing to sacrifice Czechoslovakia, in part, because of his fear that the Luftwaffe could destroy London; however, in the autumn of 1937 Chamberlain seemed to harbour little fear of the Japanese Navy. During the entire time that he was Prime Minister Chamberlain confided in his two maiden sisters, Hilda and Ida, through regular correspondence, usually every fortnight. These frequent, sometimes indiscreet, letters were not published until 2005. Chamberlain's letter to Hilda dated 9 January 1938 indicates his willingness to use the Royal Navy to intimidate Japan.

> Then there were freak 'incidents' in the Far East and our relations with U.S.A. to deal with. I am trying to jolly them along with a view to making some sort of joint (or at least 'parallel') naval action. They are incredibly slow and have missed innumerable buses, '*e puor se muore*'! I do wish the Japs would beat up an American or two! But of course the little d–v–ls are too cunning for that, & we may eventually have to act alone & hope the Yanks will follow before it's too late.[38]

The diary of Sir Alexander Cadogan, who was then the permanent undersecretary of the Foreign Office, throws some light on Chamberlain's surprisingly belligerent attitude.

> Friday, 7 January

> P.M. sent for me about 3:45 … on the Far East, had to show him press report of fresh outrage in Shanghai. Asked if I should be content with simple apology and [I] suggested time had come to tell the Americans we must do *something* (e.g. announce naval preparations) and ask whether they will take 'parallel' action. He agreed and I sent off telegram.[39]

Cadogan's telegram almost certainly went to Sir Ronald Lindsay, the British Ambassador to the US. What is astounding is that Chamberlain was willing to take such bold action without consulting the Admiralty.

Unknown to Chamberlain or Cadogan, a few weeks earlier, the Chief of Naval Operations of the US Navy had recommended to President Roosevelt a total naval blockade of Japan. Well before Pearl Harbor, William D. Leahy was among the most highly regarded admirals in the US Navy. In 1942 he became Chairman of the Joint Chiefs of Staff. In his memoir published five years after the war Leahy revealed his reaction to the sinking of *Panay*.

> That same day [24 September 1942] Secretary Hull asked me to come over to see him. ... We recalled the time four [sic] years before when I had advocated blockading Japan following the bombing of the gunboat *Panay*. Hull said his failure to take aggressive action against Tokyo was due to his knowledge that popular feeling would not support any action that might cause Japan to make war on the United States at that time. I remember disagreeing with him strongly...[40]

In 1938 the Japanese Navy was not prepared to fight the combined fleets of Britain and the US. It is worth speculating on what the outcome of a joint Anglo-American naval blockade of Japan would have been. In that event Captain Leach and HMS *Cumberland* would have almost certainly been involved.

At 11.20 London time, on 28 September 1938, the Admiralty ordered the full mobilisation of the British fleet. The Munich Crisis, as it is known, was precipitated by Hitler's threatened invasion of Czechoslovakia, supposedly for the purpose of repatriating German-speaking Czechs. Hitler's real objective was the subjugation of the entire country. Late in the crisis Chamberlain decided he would pay almost any price to avoid war with Germany. Shortly after his return to London on 24 September, following his second meeting with Hitler at Godesberg, Chamberlain had received a secret report from Ambassador Joseph P. Kennedy stating that Germany had the means of destroying London, Paris and Prague. The author of the report, Charles A. Lindbergh, had been badly duped on two brief visits to Germany, but at the time Lindbergh's reputation as an authority on military aviation was so high that the report was never challenged by Kennedy or Chamberlain.

At the beginning of the crisis HMS *Cumberland* was at a North China port some 200 miles north, northwest of Wei-Hai-Wei. Even before the Admiralty's mobilisation of 28 September, Captain Leach was ordered to proceed to Hong Kong via Wei-Hai-Wei. Shore parties were recalled from as far away as Peking before *Cumberland* could sail. On 23 September Captain Leach received orders to leave Hong Kong for England on 28 September. The next day he received an order to leave for England two days earlier. The Admiralty considered the Munich Crisis serious indeed.

By 30 September the crisis, for all intents and purposes, was over. On that day British Prime Minister Neville Chamberlain and French Premier Edouard Daladier signed the infamous Munich Accord that gave Hitler the right to march his army into the Sudetenland and thereby sever the Czechoslovakians' most important line of fortifications from the remainder of their now defenceless country.

Cumberland was refuelled and restocked at Singapore before her long passage home via Colombo, Ismailia, Aden, the Suez Canal, Malta and Gibraltar. She finally reached Chatham on the River Medway on 2 November. She secured to the strains of 'D'ye Ken John Peel'. Captain Leach's proud ship was immediately taken into dry-dock for a refit that would take her through the winter months, after which she would have a new company under a new captain.

Leach's tour of duty as captain of the *Cumberland* had been highly successful, perhaps the most satisfying appointment of his career. The final evaluation of his performance speaks for itself:

26 Sep. 38

An officer with the very highest ideals. He has produced a very high tone in his officers and men. Everyone respects him. He unfortunately suffers deafness which, although a handicap, has not seriously affected his duties in any way. Most loyal and helpful, I have lost him with great regret. He is most efficient and hard working. Has a fine figure, is very athletic and is a gentleman in every way. He is perhaps too inclined to be quiet and self effacing. Has been popular everywhere.

Sgd. Vice Admiral Sir Percy Noble[41]

Chapter V

Director of Naval Ordnance

In early 1939 Britain embarked on a massive programme to expand the Navy. The naval staff were very busy over the Naval Estimates for presentation to Parliament early in March.

> They were the largest on record in peacetime, £147,779,000. This huge total being brought about by the years of false economy and neglect to which the Navy had been subjected. No fewer than 200 warships of all types were under construction, and since 1935 the production of guns and armour had gone up 500 per cent and fire control and director gear by 900 per cent. Included in the building programme were two capital ships, *King George V* and *Prince of Wales*; 1 aircraft carrier; 4 cruisers; 16 destroyers; and 22 escort vessels – 20 of the latter being the little ships of the 'Hunt Class'... The personnel were also being increased by 14,000 to a total of 133,000.[42]

The ordnance required for this expansion exceeded any previous peacetime requirements. The naval guns came in a bewildering array of calibres. The battleships and the older battle cruisers were equipped with 16-inch, 15-inch, and 13.5-inch calibre guns. The new King George V class were being equipped with 14-inch calibre guns. Heavy cruisers were equipped with a single standard gun of 8-inch calibre. Light cruisers were equipped with six different models of 6-inch calibre guns bearing the designations Mark XVIII, XVI, XII, XI★, XI and VII.

There was also a 5.5-inch calibre gun. In 1939 the only ships in the Royal Navy with 5.5-inch calibre guns were the battlecruiser *Hood*, which had twelve, and the aircraft carrier *Hermes*, which had six. Flotilla leaders and destroyers were equipped with three different guns of 4.7-inch calibre, Mark I, Mark II, and Mark XII. Four-inch calibre guns were used as the secondary armament in battlecruisers and monitors. In 1939 British naval ordnance also included heavy and light anti-aircraft guns, anti-submarine howitzers, stick bombs and torpedoes.

For the period 1939–1940 Captain John C. Leach was Director of Naval Ordnance responsible for all policy in the Royal Navy relating to guns, gun mountings, magazines, torpedoes and electrical fittings for guns. Leach found himself in an unprecedented situation. Because of the peacetime expansion of the Royal Navy there was already an increased demand for new guns including their complex loading systems and their equally complex director systems. He had been Director for less than a year when the Second World War started, accelerating the demand for new ordnance enormously. The whole ordnance operation was well within range of the enemy's air force but fortunately, at least during the first nine months of the war, the Luftwaffe did not attack naval ordnance manufacturers, naval depots or shipyards.

Three years earlier there had been serious debate over the calibre of the guns to be installed in the new King George V class battleships. While Leach was not involved in that debate, he certainly knew about it. Churchill had initiated it with a vigorous caveat to the First Lord of the Admiralty. On 1 August 1936 he wrote to Sir Samuel Hoare:

> It is very civil of you to attach any importance to my opinion, and prime facie there is a case. I cannot answer the argument about the long delay involved. Once again we alone are injured by treaties. I cannot doubt that a far stronger ship could be built with three triple 16-inch gun turrets in a 35,000 ton hull than any combination of 14-inch. Not only would she be a better ship, but she would be rated a better ship and a more powerful token of naval power by everyone, including those who serve in her. Remember the Germans get far better results out of their guns per calibre than we do. They throw a heavier shell farther and more accurately. The answer is a big punch. Not only is there an enormous increase in the weight of a broadside,

but in addition the explosive charge of a 16-inch shell must be far larger than that of a 14-inch. If you can get through the armour it is worth while doing something inside with the explosion.

... Nothing would induce me to succumb to 14-inch if I were in your shoes. The Admiralty will look rather silly if they are committed to two 14-inch-gun ships and both Japan and the United States go in for 16-inch a few months later. I should have thought it quite possible to lie back and save six months in construction. It is terrible deliberately to build British battleships costing £7,000,000 apiece that are not the strongest in the world! As old Fisher used to say, 'The British Navy always travels first class.'[43]

Churchill lost this debate. It is interesting to speculate on what might have happened had *Prince of Wales* been equipped with nine 16-inch guns instead of ten 14-inch guns.

In 1937 the Japanese laid down the two largest and most heavily armed battleships that would ever be built by any naval power. The *Yamoto* and the *Musashi*, which were completed in 1941 or early 1942, had a standard displacement of 63,700 tons, a length of 863 feet and nine 18.1-inch guns in three turrets. Their powerful main batteries were never to be used against any British or American capital ships and they were both sunk by American carrier aircraft during the last twelve months of the war.

During the time that Leach served as Director of Naval Ordnance, his sphere of responsibility included all anti-aircraft guns. In 1939–1940 the standard light anti-aircraft guns used by the Royal Navy were the Mark VI 2-pounder pom-poms with eight barrels and the Mark VII 2-pounder pom-poms with four barrels. While they could be deadly at close range, their effective range was limited. In 1939 the finest anti-aircraft gun in the world was manufactured in Sweden by A.B. Bofors. The Bofors 40mm anti-aircraft guns L/60 in a double mounting would have given British capital ships formidable defensive fire power against both German and Japanese torpedo bombers. However, availability was severely limited. In 1939/40 the Bofors guns were only produced in any quantity in Sweden. After the German occupations of Denmark and Norway in 1940 it became impossible to obtain them from Swedish sources.

From 3 September 1939 until 10 May 1940, Churchill was First Lord of the Admiralty, and was therefore deeply involved in all aspects of the Royal Navy including naval ordnance. It was perhaps fortunate for

Leach that the DNO's headquarters was at Bath; he was thus far enough removed from the First Lord to avoid any serious clashes. Instead, Churchill busied himself with coming up with fanciful ideas involving naval operations or modifications of existing ships, which he would invariably send to the First Sea Lord in the form of a minute, such as that dated 21 October 1939. Churchill proposed the creation of a force of six battleships that would be able to withstand a 1,000-lb armour-piercing bomb. This would be achieved by laying flat armour of reinforced steel, having a thickness of six or seven inches, over all the exposed decks of HMS *Queen Elizabeth* and at least five other vessels. To compensate for the enormous increase in weight two turrets from each ship would be removed, reducing the armament of *Queen Elizabeth* and the other five ships from eight 15-inch guns to four. The seriousness of Churchill's proposal can be gleaned from the language of the minute:

> Let us therefore concentrate on having five or six vessels which are not afraid of the air, and therefore can work in narrow waters, and keep the high-class stuff for the outer oceans. Pull the guns out and plaster the decks with steel. This is the war proposition of 1940.[44]

This sounds more like a directive than a mere proposition; nevertheless, he solicited the advice of three naval advisers, one of whom was Captain Leach. Churchill clearly considered the matter to be urgent:

> All this ought to be put in motion Monday, and enough information should be provided to enable us to take far reaching decisions not later than Thursday. On that day let us have Controller, D.N.C. and D.N.O. and shift our fighting from the side of a ship to the top.[45]

The Controller was Rear Admiral Sir Bruce Fraser KBE CB, the DNC was Sir Stanley V. Goodall, KCB, OBE, Director of Naval Construction and the DNO was, of course, Captain John C. Leach, MVO. On Thursday 26 October 1939, Fraser, Goodall and Leach joined Churchill at Admiralty House 'to take far reaching decisions'. It is likely that the First Sea Lord Admiral of the Fleet Sir Dudley Pound was also present.

It can be assumed that Churchill made an extremely forceful case for modifications to the *Queen Elizabeth* and the other five ships. Pound may or may not have opposed Churchill, but the three others apparently took a strong stand against him. In the end the whole idea was quietly dropped. Churchill regretted the decision forever after. In *The Gathering Storm*, the first volume of his six-volume work on the Second World War, he wrote of his deep disappointment that he was never able to achieve his objective of 'very heavily deck-armoured ships' that could withstand air and underwater attacks better than any other vessel afloat.

Being Director of Naval Ordnance was difficult for Leach partly because of the huge size of his department, which required constant travelling, and partly because Britain's two chief manufacturers of ordnance were behind the times. These venerable companies were Harland & Wolff Ltd in Belfast, Northern Ireland, and Vickers-Armstrongs Ltd in Newcastle upon Tyne. Neither company was capable of producing a short or medium range anti-aircraft gun that could compete with the Bofors 40mm gun.

Five years after the war Captain Stephen Roskill RN became Britain's official naval historian and in 1976 the second volume of his history entitled *Naval Policy Between the Wars II: The Period of Rearmament 1930–1939* was published. In it he makes no mention of Captain Leach; however, he does criticise the Naval Ordnance Department for its failure to provide the Royal Navy with a better gun control system for long-range anti-aircraft guns.

The truth was that as long ago as the late 1920s the Admiralty had gone for the wrong sort of control system – one in which enemy aircraft movements were in effect guessed instead of being actually *measured* and the measured results used to provide the required control data. This latter called a 'tachymetric system' was the proper answer and in the letter already quoted Chatfield (First Sea Lord 1933–1938) said that he realised that this was so. The Admiralty's Director of Scientific Research C.S. (later Sir Charles) Wright was strongly of the same opinion, and in 1937 he circulated a damning critique of the existing long-range control system. But the plain truth was that the earlier mistake could not be rectified quickly, and that British designers and the light engineering industry had fallen far behind foreign countries in this respect. By 1938 the DSR (Director of Scientific Research, Admiralty) was describing the current state of affairs as 'wholly unsatisfactory' and the existing system as 'a menace to the service', nor could the Naval Ordnance Department, which was responsible for it, produce a convincing rebuttal of such statements.[46]

As Captain Roskill states, The Naval Ordnance Department was responsible for all naval anti-aircraft gun control systems. There were serious design problems, but there were no quick solutions because of the ineptitude of British engineers and manufacturers.

During the entire time that he served as Director of Naval Ordnance, Leach reported to Rear Admiral Sir Bruce Fraser, the Third Sea Lord and Controller of the Navy, who had been the Director himself from 1933–35. Admiral Fraser was a great sailor and gentleman, and was helpful to Leach because he fully understood the difficulties of serving as DNO. When Leach completed his assignment as DNO, Fraser wrote the evaluation that went into his permanent record.

> An officer of outstanding ability, integrity and leadership. Has carried out the responsible duties of DNO with success and a tact which has secured the best cooperation with the other departments. He is slightly deaf which does not however affect his work. Physically fit and a hard worker and clear character.[47]

Like Captain Leach, Admiral Fraser would experience a decisive battle with an enemy capital ship. On 26 December 1943, his flagship HMS *Duke of York* engaged and destroyed the German battleship *Scharnhorst*. That day Captain Leach's son Henry, then a young Lieutenant of 20, was Officer of the Quarters of 'A' Turret in *Duke of York*.

King George V, the first ship of the King George V class battleships, was completed on 1 October 1940. She was commissioned into service on the same day by Captain Wilfred Patterson, CVO,[48] about whom it has been said: 'Captain Wilfred Patterson was universally liked and respected. He was a quiet, kindly, determined man on whom we all depended.'[49] Leach and Captain Patterson were close friends. It is conceivable that the latter was consulted about the appointment of Leach, in early 1941, to command HMS *Prince of Wales*, the sister ship of *King George V*.

CHAPTER VI

THE ENEMY NAVIES

Nineteen forty-one would be the most dramatic year in Captain Leach's life. In a period of less than seven months his battleship, HMS *Prince of Wales*, would engage the pride of the German Navy, would almost engage an Italian battleship and at the end of the year would defend herself from a large and dangerous air flotilla of the Imperial Japanese Navy. Before examining those stirring events it is necessary to interrupt the narrative and take a close look at each enemy navy, commander-in-chief and naval strategy at the outset of 1941.

The German Navy

On 1 January 1941 Grand Admiral Erich Raeder was commander-in-chief of the Kriegsmarine, the German Navy. He was then 65, although photographs make him look considerably younger. In December 1938 Admiral Andrew Browne Cunningham was appointed head of a naval delegation to go to Berlin to persuade the German Navy and Hitler not to increase the size of the German U-boat fleet. Under the terms of the Anglo-German Naval Agreement of 1935 Germany had the right to build up to 100 per cent of British submarine strength but only under exceptional circumstances. In early December the German government informed His Majesty's Government that Germany intended to invoke this clause. Cunningham described his contacts with Admiral Raeder, then Commander-in-Chief of the Kriegsmarine:

> ... at 9.30 next morning [we] presented ourselves at the German Admiralty, where we were received by Admiral Raeder, a fine-looking man who made us a pleasant speech of welcome ... we conferred until 1 pm; but though the Germans gave the impression of great friendliness we soon realised we were up against a blank wall ... They entertained us for lunch at the Kaiserhof Hotel, with Raeder presiding. During the meal I attacked him on the subject, using particularly the argument of the effect upon public opinion at home. Eventually he promised that he would telephone to Hitler that afternoon to give him the substance of our conversation and ask his decision.[50]

Later that afternoon Cunningham received a message from Raeder that Hitler would not consent to any alteration of his plans to build the additional submarines. In a few months Hitler would promote Raeder to Grand Admiral of the German Fleet. Before Raeder resigned his command in January 1943, he had grown to loathe Hitler. Even though the Second World War generated considerable hatred towards not a few Nazi officers, there was mutual respect between Admiral Cunningham and Admiral Raeder. The latter would write over ten years after the war concerning the aforesaid negotiations and his impressions of Cunningham:

> The visit of the two British naval officers ended with a function at which they were my guests. Once again the fundamentally good relations between the two navies was made evident.
>   The negotiations went very smoothly and in a most friendly atmosphere. In a discussion between us after the negotiations both Admiral Cunningham and I expressed the warm hope that our countries would never be enemies again, and I am sure that he was as sincere in expressing that hope as I was.[51]

Some appraisals of Admiral Raeder have been inadequate and partial, with the emphasis on his conviction as a war criminal. Fortunately, the historian Ludovic Kennedy has written a more balanced view of the man.

The head of Hitler's navy was Erich Raeder, Grand Admiral in the German Fleet, a handsome square-faced man of 65, highly intelligent and approachable, son of a teacher of languages near Hamburg, like his parents, deeply religious. He joined the Navy in 1894, was navigator of the Kaiser's famous yacht *Hohenzollern* in 1911, then for five years was Chief Staff officer to Admiral Hipper, commanding the scouting forces. With Hipper he'd seen action on that other May day in 1916, off the coast of Jutland, when Jellicoe's Grand Fleet and Scheer's High Seas Fleet had their only rendezvous of the war and by next day twenty-four ships were at the bottom and over 6,000 British and 2,500 German sailors had died. … After Germany's defeat, the sending of the High Seas Fleet to Beatty for disposal, and the scuttling of it by Von Reuter at Scapa Flow, Raeder remembered these things. He remembered also the accusations of inactivity, even timidity that had been levelled at the High Seas Fleet.[52]

At the beginning of 1941 Raeder could look back on the previous year with satisfaction, but also with grave concerns. He had recommended and planned the Norwegian Campaign, which, despite the loss of a large number of the German Navy's destroyers, had proved a success. In September 1940 he had recommended that Operation *Sea Lion*, the invasion of Britain, about which he had always had the gravest doubts, be postponed indefinitely. Hitler had accepted his recommendation, but ignored his advice on a different front. When Hitler made his fateful decision to invade Russia in November 1940, Raeder had been the only senior member of OKW (*Oberkommando Der Wehrmarkt* – German High Command) to go on the record as being against it at the time.

Raeder was not only a student of naval strategy; he had a clear conception of an overall strategy that might well have enabled Germany to win the Second World War. He strongly recommended that in 1941 Hitler adopt a Mediterranean strategy involving the bulk of the Wehrmacht (German Army) and Luftwaffe. There is little doubt that in 1941 Germany could have quickly taken Malta and overrun Egypt, Palestine and Syria. This would have opened the door to the Middle East and all its oil riches. The next phase would have been the seizure of Iraq. Baghdad lay only slightly over 300 miles north-west of the Port of Abadan at the head of the Persian Gulf, which was where the Anglo-Iranian Oil Company had its main offices. The majority ownership of this company was held by the British Government. Since 1933 Anglo-

Iranian had a contract with the Government of Persia to extract oil from their oil fields, pipe it to Abadan and then refine and export it for sale abroad, a contract that did not expire until 1993. The Anglo-Iranian refineries were primary sources of oil for the Royal Navy, and Raeder believed that all of these countries and their oil resources were within the reach of Germany's armed forces. In such an event the possibility of a link-up with the Japanese Navy was very real.

> Admiral Raeder and the Naval High Command begged him [Hitler] to launch a major thrust at the Middle East, which at the time was well within German capabilities. British naval, air, and military power was thinly stretched over a vast area and vulnerable everywhere ... Raeder's view was that such a coup would strike the British Empire 'a deadlier blow than the taking of London'. Hitler had 150 divisions, plus most of the Luftwaffe, arrayed in Eastern Europe. Barely a quarter of these forces would have been enough to drive through to India. ... Britain and America, instead of being able to draw resources from five-sixths of the world and its oceans, would have been largely confined to an Atlantic sphere of operations. Victory, in these circumstances, would have seemed a wearily distant if not unattainable object ...[53]

When it became obvious that Hitler was obsessed with invading Russia no later than June 1941, Raeder had to revise his strategy. He believed that it would be difficult, but not impossible, for the German Navy to cut Britain's lines of communication with the outside world. To achieve this he would use a combination of long range U-boats, pocket battleships, battle cruisers, and his most powerful ship of all, the *Bismarck*. In addition he would send out auxiliary cruisers disguised as neutral merchant ships.

At the beginning of 1941 Raeder was desperately short of destroyers, although they were of little or no use as surface-raiders. He was also short of light cruisers which had the same shortcomings. Perhaps the best of his light cruisers was *Nürnberg*, but her main armament of nine 5.9-inch guns in three turrets would not suffice in any engagement with a British heavy cruiser. Her radius of action with diesel engines at 14.5 knots was only 3,800 miles. Raeder did have at his disposal three modern heavy cruisers, *Admiral Hipper*, *Prinz Eugen* and *Seydlitz* that were armed with eight 8-inch guns and had a cruising radius of 6,800 miles. He also had two pocket battleships that were less than ten years old, *Lützow* and *Admiral Scheer* that were armed with six 11-inch guns and had a cruising radius of 10,000 miles at 15 knots, and two small modern battleships, *Scharnhorst* and *Gneisenau* that were armed with nine 11-inch guns and had a cruising radius of at least 10,000 miles. Within six months Raeder would acquire two new battleships which were the largest and most powerful ever built for the German Navy. They were *Bismarck* and *Tirpitz*. These two behemoths were armed with eight 15-inch guns and had a cruising radius of over 8,000 miles.

Raeder was deadly serious about cutting Britain's lines of communications and was willing to take enormous risks with everything he had in both ships and men. During the first eighteen months of the war his ships broke out into the Atlantic through the Denmark Strait, the passageway between Greenland and Iceland, as well as the passageways east of Iceland. They then spread out into the vast reaches of the Atlantic, the South Atlantic and the Indian Ocean searching for prey.

Near the end of October 1940 the pocket-battleship *Scheer* put to sea from the small naval base at Brunsbüttel. Between then and her return to Bergen on 30 March, her captain's 48th birthday, she had sunk the 14,000-ton British armed merchant cruiser *Jervis Bay* and fourteen allied merchantmen and had taken two prizes. More significantly she had caused prolonged and serious disruption to the British convoy system and to the dispositions of the Royal Navy in the Atlantic and beyond.

In 1941 Raeder risked his only two battleships on a prolonged raid into the Atlantic. On 23 January *Scharnhorst* and *Gneisenau* under the flag of Admiral Günther Lütjens sailed from Kiel. After refuelling from one of their previously dispatched fuelling tankers in the Arctic, they passed through the Denmark Strait on the night of 3/4 February. While they had some close encounters with heavy units of the Royal Navy, they nevertheless were able to continue their mission. A few hundred miles east of Newfoundland they sank five ships from a freshly dispersed convoy. After veering as far south as the Cape Verde Island, they returned to the route of convoys between Halifax and the British Isles. In that area on 15 and 16 March they sank sixteen ships from dispersed convoys. A number of other ships under Admiral Raeder's command were also active in the Atlantic during this period. They included the heavy cruiser *Admiral Hipper* and disguised auxiliary cruisers.

When the Royal Navy intensified its efforts to locate and destroy *Scharnhorst* and *Gneisenau*, these two formidable ships took the shortest route to a friendly harbour, rather than returning through the Denmark Strait to Norway. On 22 March they sailed triumphantly into Brest.

The historian Dan van der Vet has written of their successful voyage:

When Lütjens brought his ships unharmed into Brest, Raeder's second congratulatory telegram was positively fulsome. It was richly deserved. At the end of March 1941, nineteen months into a war with the world's greatest navy, the Germans had lost only one pocket-battleship and one heavy cruiser from the major ships in their small but modern and power-ful surface fleet … Admiral Raeder and his staff could look back with considerable satisfaction on a year and a half in which an onslaught by mines, surface-ships and submarines had seriously affected the enemy's ability to fight on.[54]

This same historian gives much credit to the German Navy for what he describes as 'the superb efficiency of the German mid-ocean supply system'.[55] The aforesaid successes of the German surface-raiders could not have been accomplished without refuelling tankers and supply ships with naval stores that always seemed to appear at the right time and the right place.

Grand Admiral Raeder has been relegated to second place by most naval historians who consider his successor Admiral Karl Doenitz as the greater of the two Supreme Commanders. Yet they may have underestimated Raeder. In addition to his organisational skills that were reflected in the efficiency with which the German Navy resup-plied its surface raiders in early 1941, Raeder had demonstrated the daring of a great admiral. After the war he described the need to take risks as follows:

If we were to achieve anything worthwhile with our numerically weak naval forces, then they had to be used to the best possible purpose, with constant tactical innovations and new ideas. This required a daring strategy and a willingness to take risks on the part of Naval Operations Command, as well as skilful operational leadership by the men in com-mand of our ships at sea.[56]

Before the end of May that year, when England still stood alone, Raeder would take his greatest risk. He would order Captain Lütjens to break out into the Atlantic with Germany's greatest ship, the *Bismarck*.

The Italian Navy

At the time of Mussolini's declaration of war against Britain and France on 10 June 1940, Italy appeared to have a navy that could challenge Britain for control of the Mediterranean. At its head, Admiral Cavagnari had served as chief of staff and under-secretary for seven years which has been called 'an exceptionally lengthy period of command during the fascist regime'.[57]

On the outset of the conflict, just days before the fall of France, the Italian Navy consisted of six battleships, two modern and four of which had been rebuilt; nineteen cruisers, seven of which were 10,000 tons; over 100 smaller surface vessels and 113 submarines. Churchill has described the *Littorio* and her sister ship as 'of the latest type, mounting fifteen-inch guns'.[58]

Within the first five months of its war against Britain the Italian Navy suffered two defeats from which it never recovered. The first defeat was on 9 July 1940, less than 30 days after Mussolini's declaration of war. It became known as the Action off Calabria, a region in southern Italy sometimes referred to as the toe of the Italian boot. Earlier in July it had been decided to evacuate as many civilians from Malta as the Royal Navy could get away. These included the wives and children of British sailors who were now scattered to the four corners of the earth. Amongst the wives was Nona Byatt Cunningham, the wife of the commander-in-chief of the Mediterranean Fleet. Arrangements had also been made to remove all the Italian prisoners of war who had been brought to Malta and to bring out a considerable quantity of naval stores badly needed at Alexandria in four slow ships.

The whole operation involving one fast convoy and one slow convoy was to be carried out under cover of the whole fleet. Admiral Cunningham, the Commander-in-Chief, flew his flag in *Warspite*. Cunningham's fleet included two other battleships, *Malaya* and *Royal Sovereign*; the aircraft carrier *Eagle*; five cruisers, *Orion, Neptune, Sydney*,

Gloucester and *Liverpool*; and seventeen destroyers. The action is best described in Cunningham's' own words:

> The fleet sailed from Alexandria late in the evening of July 7th, all ships being clear of the harbour by midnight … throughout July 8th all units of the fleet met with fairly heavy bombing attacks by Italian aircraft from the Dodecanese. The only casualty, but a serious one, was a hit on the *Gloucester*'s bridge, which killed Captain F.R. Garside and seventeen others, and necessitated the ship being steered and fought from the after control position … at dawn on July 9th the *Eagle* flew off three aircraft to reconnoitre. However, it was about 7:30 a.m. that another flying boat from Malta again reported the enemy fleet to the westward at distance from us of about a hundred and forty-five miles … further reports during the forenoon from the flying-boats and the *Eagle*'s aircraft showed that an Italian fleet of at least two battleships, twelve cruisers and numerous destroyers were out …
>
> Vice Admiral Tovey's four ships (the cruisers except for *Gloucester*) were about ten miles ahead of *Warspite*. About ten miles astern of us came the *Royal Sovereign* and *Malaya* screened by nine destroyers … At 3.08 the *Neptune*, Captain Rory O'Conor, sighted the Italian heavy ships, and was the first British warship to signal 'Enemy battle fleet in sight' in the Mediterranean since the time of Nelson … the great moment came when at 3.53 *Warspite* opened fire on the leading enemy battleship at a range of 26,000 yards. Both the Italian battleships replied. They shot well and straddled us at this great range; but the culminating point of the engagement soon came. The *Warspite*'s shooting was consistently good. I had been watching the great splashes of our 15-inch salvos straddling the target when at 4 p.m., I saw the great orange-coloured flash of a heavy explosion at the base of the enemy flagship's funnels. It was followed by an upheaval of smoke, and I knew that she had been heavily hit at the prodigious range of thirteen miles …
>
> This was too much for the Italian Admiral, my old friend Riccardi, whom I had entertained in the *Hood* in 1938 … His ships turned away …[59]
>
> A short time later an observer from one of *Warspite*'s aircraft reported 'that the enemy fleet was left in considerable confusion and that all units were making off at high speed to the west and south-west towards the Straits of Messina and Augusta.'[60]

The *Warspite's* hit on the Italian flagship *Giulio Cesare* at 26,000 yards was a record not broken by any other battleship in action at sea during the entire war. From then until Italy's surrender over three years later the Italian admirals never allowed any of their battleships to get within range of a British battleship. The significance of this victory was not lost on the naval historian Correlli Barnett:

> The Royal Navy had asserted its moral domination in that first major encounter off Calabria when Cunningham's ships for all their technical inferiority steamed straight for the enemy, who, in the C-in-C's words, as soon as *Warspite* hit him in the ribs at 26,000 yards … screamed for a smoke screen, ordered 25 knots and turned 90 degrees away.[61]

The second victory by the Royal Navy over the Italians in 1940 inflicted much greater losses. This was the famous Fleet Air Arm attack on the Italian Fleet supposedly safely ensconced in harbour at Taranto where 21 Swordfish aircraft from the carrier *Illustrious* sunk or disabled three Italian battleships on the night of 11/12 November. More will be said about the significance of this action in a later chapter, but suffice to say that when Cunningham detached *Illustrious* (flying the flag of Rear Admiral Lyster) and her screen of four cruisers and four destroyers to her flying-off position about 170 miles south-east of Taranto, he made the following signal to Lyster:

> Good luck then to your lads and their enterprise. Their success may well have most important bearing on the course of the war in the Mediterranean.[62]

Cunningham's words were understated. Shortly afterwards there was a major shakeup in the top Italian Navy commanders. Admiral Riccardi replaced Admiral Cavagnari as Undersecretary of State and Head of Supermarina. Admiral Iachino replaced Admiral Campioni as Fleet Commander-in-Chief.

Riccardi was not one of the great admirals of the Second World War. He lacked Raeder's strategic vision and willingness to take risks with his battleships. From the beginning of his tenure as Head of Supermarina Riccardi's primary object was to safeguard his battleships. He kept them in secure harbours as far as possible from British bombers except for occasional sorties that were carefully planned to lure British heavy ships within range of Italian torpedo bombers and submarines.

The Imperial Japanese Navy

Actual hostilities between the Royal Navy and the Imperial Japanese Navy did not commence until 7 December, which was 8 December in Singapore. While archival evidence is lacking (Those of the Japanese were presumably destroyed in air raids on Tokyo), the circumstantial evidence is compelling that the Japanese Naval General Staff and Admiral Isoroku Yamamoto – Commander-in-Chief of the Combined Fleet – had devised a strategy to drive the British out of Hong Kong, Borneo, Malaya, Singapore and Burma and the Dutch out of the Netherland East Indies, well over a year in advance.

Three events in Europe convinced the Japanese warlords that a quick and decisive victory was achievable over the colonial powers that heretofore had possessed most of the natural resources of the South Pacific: the collapse of Holland, the fall of France and the blockade of Britain. In the Far East a minor naval encounter on 11 November 1940 resulted in a major intelligence coup. On that date the German auxiliary cruiser *Atlantis*, disguised as a Dutch merchant ship, intercepted the Blue Funnel steamer *Automedon* off the Nicobar Islands. When the British ship continued to transmit distress signals, *Atlantis* opened fire with her 5.9-inch guns. Before the *Automedon's* radio was silenced, the *Atlantis'* gun fire had killed the *Automedon's* captain and six others. Twelve members of the crew were wounded. A special admiralty courier was also temporarily disabled and was therefore unable to destroy top secret documents that were intended for Air Chief Marshal Sir Robert Brooke-Popham, Commander-in-Chief, Far East. The German boarders got into the ship's strong room, blew the safe and seized the documents.

The following month these documents were passed on to senior officers of the Japanese Navy. The most revealing was a Chiefs of Staff report which concluded that Hong Kong, French Indo-China, Malaya and the Netherlands East Indies were indefensible, a conclusion that had been approved by the British war cabinet on 15 August 1940. The fate of these documents became known in the UK by the end of the year, but neither Brooke-Popham, the British public nor any of Britain's allies were informed of their loss. Finally in 1980 they became public knowledge when Magic Intelligence decrypts were declassified by the United States National Security Agency. They revealed a signal from the Japanese attaché in Berlin that described the whole affair.

In the post-war years it became a matter of dogma in certain Japanese intellectual circles that Japan was forced into the war by the American oil embargo. This polemic lacks any real substance. The Japanese Navy's war strategy was in place long before President Roosevelt's famous oil embargo of July 1941 after which the Netherlands then cancelled all of their oil contracts with Japan. The Combined Fleet Commander of the Imperial Japanese Navy would complete his operational plans shortly thereafter, but his strategy was already well in place.

The attack on Pearl Harbor represents one of the most devastating surprise attacks in naval history. Whether the decision to attack was made before or after the decision to overrun the Netherlands East Indies is not clear. What is clear is that the purpose of the attack was the destruction of the US Pacific Fleet, which among other benefits would protect the eastern flank of the Southern Operation.

Yamamoto was born in 1894 in Nagaoko, the son of a schoolmaster. In 1904 he passed out of the Japanese Naval Academy just in time for the Russo-Japanese War. He fought at the Battle of Tsushima Strait; he lost two fingers from his left hand and was wounded in the leg. In 1919 he was sent to the US to study English, living in Boston he learned to play poker with its 'mixture of bluff, luck and anticipation'.[63] The game influenced his views on naval strategy.

In 1926 Yamamoto returned to the US as naval attaché at the Japanese Embassy in Washington. In his two years there he came in contact with numerous US Navy officers, and while he never held illusions about American industrial power, he developed 'a low opinion of the US Navy which he described as a club for golfers and bridge players.'[64] In contrast his participation at the 1930 London Naval Conference as a rear admiral brought him in contact with numerous Royal Navy officers, and he seemed to hold the Royal Navy in a higher regard than the US Navy because prior to the First World War the former had been something of a role model for the Imperial Japanese Navy.

In October 1933 he took command of the 1st Carrier Division and in 1935 he became vice admiral and vice-minister of the Japanese Navy. By then he was an ardent supporter of air power and unlike some of his colleagues he lacked faith in battleships. In 1939 Yamamoto was promoted to Commander-in-Chief of the Combined Fleet, and by 1 January 1941 he was the single most influential admiral in the Imperial Japanese Navy. In 1989 historian H.P. Willmott wrote:

> Since the end of the Second World War western histories have for the most part carried as an unquestioned fact the relative moderation of the Imperial Navy, its being dragged unwillingly into war by a boorish army and its misgivings about the outcome of a war with the US. This portrayal of the Imperial Navy has rested in large measure upon the known views of its Combined Fleet Commander … but the process whereby the opinions of Yamamoto have become the alibi of the Imperial Navy is distinctly misleading.[65]

While few archives of the Imperial Japanese Navy survived the war, some of Yamamoto's private letters did. The American historian Gordon W. Prange found a letter dated 10 December 1940, which Admiral Yamamoto wrote to one of his closest confidants, Vice Admiral Shigetaro Shimada.

> The probability is great that the launching of our operation against the Netherlands Indies will lead to an early commencement of war with America, and since Britain and Holland will side with America, our operations against the Netherlands Indies are almost certain to develop into a war with America, Britain and Holland before those operations are half over. Consequently we should not launch out on the southern operation unless we are at least prepared to face such an eventuality and are, moreover, adequately equipped …[66]

Prange was arguably the leading American scholar on the Pearl Harbor disaster. During the Second World War he served as an officer in the US Naval Reserves and from October 1946 to June 1951 he was chief of General Douglas MacArthur's G-2 Historical Section. While teaching at the University of Maryland, he devoted 37 years of his life to researching and writing his magnum opus, *At Dawn We Slept – The Untold Story of Pearl Harbor*, for which Prange had personally interviewed virtually every surviving Japanese officer who took part in the attack. He was rewarded for his diligence when he learned from Japanese sources that it was Admiral Yamamoto's custom to write and sign both an original draft and a final letter in communicating with most of his colleagues. Prange also learned that Yamamoto never dictated these letters; he invariably brushed out both the original draft and the final letter in his own hand, writing in a style which virtually amounted to a code.

In 1964 the family of Captain Shigeru Fujii, a member of Yamamoto's staff, found a draft of one of Yamamoto's letters among Captain Fujii's personal effects. They presented it to the Historical Department of the Japanese Self-Defense Force. Inevitably, it came to Prange's attention.

An intensely serious man sat at his desk in his cabin aboard the 32,000 ton battleship *Nagato* as she swung at anchor at Hashirajima in Hiroshima Bay on January 7, 1941. One can picture this man as he placed a piece of paper before him, grasped his brush, and marshalled his thoughts. Then when the spirit moved him, he wrote in quick, bold strokes one of the most historically revealing letters in the annals of the Imperial Japanese Navy ...[67]

So bearing in mind that this man was a law unto himself, let us return to that cold winter's day of January 7, 1941. In his cabin Yamamoto sat composing a long letter to Oikawa. [Admiral Koshiro Oikawa was appointed Navy Minister on 4 September 1940. He controlled personnel appointments for the Pearl Harbor striking force.] As he wrote an observer might note that his left hand lacked the fore and middle fingers – lost in the Battle of Tsushima against the Russians in May 1905.

The brush splashed forcefully across the paper. In view of the bleak international situation, wrote Yamamoto, the time has come for the Navy 'to devote itself seriously to war preparations' because 'a conflict with the United States and Great Britain is inevitable.'

Yamamoto emphasised that the Japanese Navy should 'fiercely attack and destroy the US main fleet at the outset of the war, so that the morale of the US Navy and her people' would 'sink to the extent that it could not be recovered.'

...Gathering momentum, he insisted that 'we should do our very best at the outset of the war with the United States ... to decide the fate of the war on the very first day.' Next, Yamamoto outlined his two-part 'operational plan':'1. In case the majority of the enemy's main force is at Pearl Harbor, attack it vigorously with our air force, and blockade the harbor. 2. If the enemy remains outside the harbor, apply the same method as above.'

He also informed Oikawa what forces he had in mind and their assignments: the First and Second Carrier divisions, or the latter alone at a pinch, in order 'to launch a forced or surprise attack with all their air strength, risking themselves on a moonlight night or at dawn' …[68]

Nor did Yamamoto lose sight of Japan's principal objective. A 'forestalling and surprise attack on enemy air forces in the Philippines and Singapore should definitely be made almost at the same time as the attack against Hawaii.'[69]

Admiral Yamamoto's two largest battleships, *Musashi* and *Yamato*, which were the most massive battleships ever built, were still being completed at the time the Pearl Harbor strike force left Japanese waters. Even without these two super battleships, Yamamoto commanded a large and balanced fleet to carry out his plans to destroy the US Pacific Fleet. *The Oxford Companion to World War II* itemises the Japanese Navy's strength in ships on 7 December 1941 as follows.

Battleships	10
Aircraft Carriers	10
Heavy Cruisers	18
Light Cruisers	20
Destroyers	112
Submarines	65
Others	156
Total	391[70]

This same source states that it had 'a front line strength of about 1,750 fighters, torpedo-bombers, and bombers, and some 530 flying boats and float planes for reconnaissance missions.'[71]

For both the Royal and US Navy the Imperial Japanese Navy presented a formidable adversary. Before the Second World War the conventional wisdom was that the decisive battle would be fought in the Western Pacific between the main Japanese battle fleet and that of the US, and it was assumed that the battleship would have the dominant role. The risk that Japanese carrier aircraft posed to American battleships at their moorings in Pearl Harbor was therefore terribly underestimated, and the risk that land-based Japanese torpedo bombers posed to British battleships operating in the South China Sea was barely considered.

In January 1941 England stood alone. She could (probably) repulse any German invasion, but she could not hope to defeat Germany on the Continent without either Russia or America as her ally. Stalin had no intention of coming to England's aid. He loathed British capitalism as much or more than he loathed Germany's National Socialism, and before 1941 his secret agents had already penetrated MI5. His most valuable agent was Harold Adrian Russell Philby, a graduate of Trinity College, Cambridge.

In the US, Franklin Roosevelt had just been elected president for an unprecedented third term. He was prepared to do everything in his power to help Britain prevail, but he could not act without the consent of Congress. Because Roosevelt wanted a first-hand report on the situation in England and above all whether her people had the will to win, he sent his most trusted adviser to London. Churchill had never heard of Harry Lloyd Hopkins, but he soon forged a remarkable friendship with this frail, ill American. The two men spent time together at 10 Downing Street and at Chequers. In the middle of January Churchill took Hopkins to Scapa Flow to inspect the Home Fleet. It was one of the coldest winters on record in Scotland and Hopkins suffered terribly from the cold; he never complained.

On the night of Wednesday 15 January, Hopkins was the guest of honour at a dinner in the wardroom of the battleship HMS *Nelson*. The Royal Navy officers whom he met that freezing night included Vice Admiral Lancelot Holland and Captain William George Tennant. Captain Leach knew both men and before the year was over he would witness the destruction of each friend's ship in separate engagements at opposite ends of the earth.

Churchill and Hopkins spent their last night in Scotland in Glasgow. Before that night was over Churchill would learn Hopkins' true feelings about the British nation. Churchill's doctor, Sir Charles Wilson, later Lord Moran, heard every word that Hopkins spoke. He recorded the following in his diary:

On the return journey, Tom Johnston dined us at the Station Hotel at Glasgow, and I sat next to Harry Hopkins, an unkempt figure. After a time he got up and turning to the P.M. said: 'I suppose you wish to know what I am going to say to President Roosevelt on my return. Well, I am going to quote you one verse from the Book of Books, in the truth of which

Mr Johnston's mother and my own Scottish mother were brought up: 'Whither thou goest, I will go; and where thou lodgest, I will lodge; thy people shall be my people, and thy God my God!' Then he added very quietly, 'Even to the end.'

I was surprised to find the P.M. in tears. He knew what it meant. Even to us the words seemed like a rope thrown to a drowning man.[72]

Chapter VII

HMS *Prince of Wales*

On 1 January 1937, for the first time in over ten years, two battleships for the Royal Navy were laid down by Britain's premier shipbuilders. At Newcastle upon Tyne, Vickers-Armstrong Ltd laid down HMS *King George V*. On the west coast, at Birkenhead, Cammell Laird & Co. Ltd laid down HMS *Prince of Wales*. These two were the first of a class of five battleships. They would be the last battleships Britain would build in the Second World War. *King George V* was originally intended to be named after the reigning sovereign, but the new King, George VI, insisted that she should be named in honour of his father, King George V. The initial ship's name determined the name of the class. Hence this class of battleships would always be called King George V class battleships.

By the Washington Naval Treaty of 1922 the displacement of HMS *King George V* and HMS *Prince of Wales* could not exceed 35,000 tons. The ships' main armament consisted of ten 14-inch guns arranged in three turrets. Their secondary armament consisted of sixteen 5.25-inch guns that could be used against both surface and aircraft targets. The 14-inch guns were a new model with an effective range greater than the 16-inch guns of the *Nelson* and *Rodney*, which were the last battleships to be built before *King George V* and *Prince of Wales*.

In May of 1937 Neville Chamberlain succeeded Stanley Baldwin as prime minister. During his three years in office Chamberlain took little interest in the Royal Navy, and was in fact responsible for limiting the naval estimates for 1938. Duff Cooper was First Lord of the Admiralty for most of 1938, and his diary for 23 January reveals the Chamberlain Government's frugality with the Royal Navy.

> I had a discouraging letter from the Chancellor of the Exchequer [Sir John Simon] last week. He wants us to reduce our proposed estimates by £6,000,000 and I don't see how it can be done. Meanwhile the Chiefs of Staff are preparing a report for the Committee of Imperial Defence to the effect that our rearmament programme is quite inadequate to meet the dangers with which we are faced, and we must either increase the scale of it, or reduce our liabilities by making friends with one of our potential enemies ...[73]

On 2 July 1938 Prime Minister Chamberlain made a major speech on defence and rearmament at a government rally at Kettering:

> I am not sure that the public fully realises the gigantic effort we are making in this defence programme. Our shipbuilding yards have a tremendous number of warships to build. Orders for new warships that we have placed since April, 1935, amount to something like half the tonnage of the entire fleet as it existed at that time.
>   We are beginning to see the results today in those powerful new cruisers and destroyers, along with a lot of smaller craft, which are joining the fleet in a continuous stream. Our enormous programme of battleship construction and reconstruction will ensure our continued supremacy in capital ships.[74]

His last sentence was at best wishful thinking. The Admiralty could no longer be confident that the Royal Navy maintained supremacy in capital ships. Britain and Germany were then engaged in an arms race to see which country could produce the better battleship; in July 1938 the outcome was far from certain. The German naval architects, ordnance experts and shipbuilders were superb, and two new German battleships, the *Bismarck* and the *Tirpitz*, were laid down in 1936. Upon their completion they would prove to be the finest battleships in the world, and the Royal Navy had only two ships that might be able to engage them, though not on equal terms: the *King George V* and *Prince of Wales*. The vital question was whether these two battleships would be ready in time; they had to be built, worked up (which took around eight months) and crewed with 1,500 men.

A declaration of war between Great Britain and Germany went into effect at 11am London time on Sunday 3 September 1939 when Germany failed to comply with Britain's ultimatum to withdraw all of her forces from Polish soil following a massive invasion on 1 September. Shortly after midday Churchill gave his first speech of the Second World War.

> In this solemn hour it is a consolation to recall and to dwell upon our repeated efforts for peace. All have been ill-starred, but all have been faithful and sincere. This is the highest moral valve – and not only moral valve, but practical valve – of the present time, because the wholehearted concurrence of scores of millions of men and women, whose co-operation is indispensable and whose comradeship and brotherhood are indispensable, is the only foundation upon which the trial and tribulation of modern war can be endured and surmounted.[75]

Before his speech Chamberlain had sent him a note asking him to come to his room as soon as the debate died down. When they met, the Prime Minister offered Churchill the Admiralty as well as a seat in the War Cabinet. Realising that time was of the essence Churchill sent word to the Admiralty that he would take charge forthwith and would arrive at Whitehall at 6pm. Immediately upon receipt of Churchill's message the Admiralty sent out the famous signal to the Fleet. 'Winston is back.'[76]

Churchill was as well aware of the urgent need to complete HMS *King George V* and HMS *Prince of Wales*. He was incensed by reports from Vickers-Armstrongs and Cammell Laird indicating that neither shipbuilder could comply with its contract dates. On 8 September Churchill minuted the First Sea Lord Sir Dudley Pound.

> A supreme effort must be made to finish *King George V* and *Prince of Wales* by their contract dates. The peace-time habit of contractors in booking orders and executing them when they please cannot be allowed to continue in time of war. Advise me of the penalties that may be enforced, in order that a case may be stated, if necessary, to the Law Officers of the Crown. Advise me also of the limiting factors. I suppose, as usual,

to gun-mountings. It must be considered a marked failure by all concerned if these ships are not finished by their contract dates ... It is no
use the contractors saying it cannot be done. I have seen it done when full
pressure is applied and every resource and contrivance utilised. In short,
we must have K.G.V. by July 1940 and P. of W. three months later. The
ships we need to win the war with must be in commission in 1940.[77]

The First Lord of the Admiralty was asking the impossible. Nevertheless
King George V was commissioned on 1 October 1940 only three months
after her contract date. The *Prince of Wales* was not officially accepted
by the Royal Navy until 31 March 1941. Some of the delays were due
to the complexities inherent in her turret design 'with its attendant
ammunition supply arrangements ... In all, there were about 3,000
intricate working parts in the quadruple turrets.'[78] In the case of
Prince of Wales, delay was due in part to enemy action. In August 1940
the Luftwaffe's strategic plan was to destroy the Royal Air Force and
gain total daylight air supremacy over the British Isles. Their attacks,
therefore, were directed primarily at airfields, sector stations, radar
installations and aircraft factories. Through aerial photographs the
Germans learned that the *Prince of Wales* was being built at the Cammell
Laird shipyards at Birkenhead near Liverpool within range of German
bombers. It is unclear whether Admiral Erich Raeder, Commander-in-
Chief of German Naval Forces, requested the Luftwaffe to bomb and, if
possible, destroy *Prince of Wales*. In any event in August 1940 the Germans
raided Liverpool and Birkenhead. A heavy bomb 'exploded underwater
about six feet from the port side of the bilge keel below the vicinity of
the aft 5.25-inch guns.'[79] The damage to the hull was serious enough to
result in *Prince of Wales* being towed into a dry-dock where the damaged
hull plates were replaced.

On 28 January 1941 the *Prince of Wales* steamed to Rosyth on the
east coast of Scotland with two of her four propellers lashed down on
the upper deck. It was there that her completion and final fitting out
took place. She was then under the command of Captain L.K. 'Turtle'
Hamilton, who was about to be promoted to Rear Admiral.

It was a proud day in the life of John Catterall Leach when he relieved
Captain Hamilton as *Prince of Wales'* commanding officer. He was taking
command of the newest and most modern battleship in the Royal Navy;
yet it was a ship that did not even have her full company of officers and

ratings, had not been fitted out with her ammunition and thousands of tons of supplies and had not yet started the eight-month breaking-in and work-up process that was essential to make certain she was ready to engage the enemy.

When Captain Leach assumed command, neither the shipbuilder nor the Admiralty fully appreciated the deficiencies that existed in the *Prince of Wales*. At least two of these deficiencies were extraordinarily serious: the main armament was prone to malfunction because of failures in the intricate loading system and the ship's ventilation system was utterly inadequate to give relief from temperatures that far exceeded 100°F in seas anywhere near the equator.

V.E. Tarrant in his book *King George V Class Battleships* has managed to bring to life each of the five ships and their captains. He wrote of Captain John C. Leach:

> Forty-six at the time he took command of the battleship, Leach, whose fate was inexorably bound to that of *Prince of Wales*, was a gun- nery specialist who was also thoroughly competent in all branches of his profession, including ship handling, slightly deaf, in the best Whale Island (gunnery school) tradition, he was nonetheless athletic, being an ace squash, racquets and tennis player. A tall, broad shouldered, bony- featured man with blue eyes, thinning reddish hair, he was completely devoid of any vestige of pomposity and was easily approachable. In an era when the relationship between officer and rating was sometimes austere, 'Jack' Leach – or 'Trunky' as he was affectionately referred to amongst the lower deck (on account of his large nose) – was able to inspire in the ship's company a devotion and willingness to serve that was outstanding. Despite being a firm disciplinarian when wrongs were committed, he was fair and transparently decent and was content to jolly people along rather than drive them.[80]

Leach eschewed playing favourites among his ship's officers, but there were clearly some that he liked more than others. Acting Lieutenant Commander George Ferguson RNVR was almost certainly one of them. Ferguson's action station was high in the superstructure where he was in charge of the air defence position. In August of that year the prominent newspaperman, H. V. Morton, boarded *Prince of Wales* to write an account of Churchill's meeting with Roosevelt at Placentia Bay off the coast of Newfoundland. Morton struck up an easy friendship with Ferguson. In his book *Atlantic Meeting*, Morton introduces Ferguson to his readers by informing them that over the mantelpiece in the ward-room Lieutenant Commander George Ferguson, in a moment of characteristic generosity, had hung an irreverent caricature of the Prince Regent by Gilroy. Morton went on to describe Ferguson as follows:

> He was probably forty but he looked no more than twenty-five. He might have appeared as he was, and at any moment, upon any stage, but prefer-ably a musical comedy stage, and have played the part of a typical British naval officer. He was almost too good to be true. He had a pink face and a pair of pale blue eyes; and I never knew him to descend from the high eyrie on which he spent his hours of duty without some amusing happening to relate or some preposterous story he had just remembered. Life was full of rich flavours for George Ferguson, and his vitality was remarkable … As he entered the wardroom, or rather as he quite uncon-sciously, made an entrance spinning his cap on a peg or a table, he brought with him an improbable air of fox-hunting … Quinn [the Surgeon Commander] told me that Ferguson had been badly smashed up in an air raid on Portsmouth. He had a fractured spine, a fractured pelvis and a collapsed lung, and no one thought it possible that he could recover. But in a remarkable short time he emerged from hospital, as bright as a pint of quicksilver, and rejoined his ship.[81]

Captain Leach had not seen the King since 1927 when the Duke and Duchess of York had made their royal tour of New Zealand and Australia. On 6 March 'King George VI toured the battleship and inspected the ship's company drawn up in divisions on the quarterdeck.'[82] It marked the first occasion King George VI had inspected one of his King George V class battleships. There is no record of the conversation between the King and *Prince of Wales'* captain. One can well imagine their pleasure in enjoying a whisky together in the wardroom.

Captain Leach and King George VI saw one another again in April at Pitreavie Castle near Rosyth. The King was making an official visit to the Commander-in-Chief for the East coast of Scotland, Admiral Sir Bertram Ramsey, who had done such magnificent work in organising the evacuation of the BEF from Dunkirk. At least one photograph of this royal visit survives. The King is shown standing in the middle of a group of thirteen Royal Navy and Army officers. Admiral Sir Bertram Ramsey is on the King's right and Captain Leach stands in the second row just behind them. It would be their final meeting.

On 31 March Leach formally accepted the handing over certificate for HMS *Prince of Wales* from John Harvey, the authorised representative of Cammell Laird & Co., Ltd. The certificate is revealing in three particulars. It was signed and delivered to Captain Leach at sea at 11.50pm on 31 March, and was accepted by him without prejudice to outstanding liabilities. That this was done at sea just before midnight suggests that Cammell Laird's personnel were working overtime on the ship up to the last moment. The phrase in the document 'without prejudice to outstanding liabilities' meant that no rights or privileges of the

Scapa Flow at the end of the Second World War. *(Courtesy of G. Gordon Nicol)*

Royal Navy were considered as thereby waived or lost except in so far as may be expressly conceded or decided. Cammell Laird's legal obligations were to complete the *Prince of Wales* in accordance with plans, specifications and other contractual obligations. Since it was soon necessary to bring specialists from another company, Vickers-Armstrongs Ltd, on board to correct malfunctions with the loading and reloading of the main guns, Cammell Laird never fully complied with its obligations.

Only seven weeks elapsed between the handing over from Cammell Laird and the date that *Prince of Wales* steamed out of Scapa Flow on her first operational mission. Seven weeks was far too short a time for her to achieve the full benefit from her working-up process; nevertheless, Leach used every available day to make *Prince of Wales* ready to join the Home Fleet. There were concentrated gunnery trials with the heavy guns and the secondary batteries firing all day and towards the end of the working-up period they continued into the night. All the while civilian technicians from Vickers-Armstrongs were in each turret correcting malfunctions; when *Prince of Wales* steamed into Scapa Flow around 19 May, they were still on board.

Leach's field was gunnery and he well knew that the best way of sinking an enemy battleship was to overwhelm her with broadsides from heavy guns. The challenge that confronted him throughout May was whether his heavy guns would malfunction during a surface engagement as the gunnery trials had not been totally reassuring. Nevertheless, on the morning of 21 May Leach informed Admiral Sir John Tovey, the Commander-in-Chief of the Home Fleet, that he considered *Prince of Wales* ready to take her place. Later that day Tovey ordered *Prince of Wales* – together with her flagship HMS *Hood* and escorted by six destroyers – out to sea to intercept the *Bismarck*. Captain Leach's first operational mission would develop into the most dramatic surface engagement of the entire war.

Chapter VIII

Battle of the Denmark Strait

Trondheim Fjord is an inlet of the Norwegian Sea indenting the coast of west central Norway for some 80 miles. The approximate location is 63°39′N, 10°49′E. Here on 22 May 1941 at 0500 Admiral Günther Lütjens of the German Navy took his squadron of two warships beyond what proved to be the point of no return. Until this time they had steamed through the Baltic Sea and along the Norwegian coast with an escort of three destroyers to deal with any enemy submarines and fighter aircraft to fend off enemy bombers. Now Lütjens was on his own.

He flew his Admiral's flag in the battleship *Bismarck*, which was accompanied by the heavy cruiser *Prinz Eugen*. The latter was a formidable warship with eight 8-inch guns in four turrets, numerous anti-aircraft guns and twelve 21-inch torpedo tubes. Her four turrets, single funnel and modern superstructure gave her a silhouette that resembled the *Bismarck*'s. She could not, however, compare with the latter, which was the most powerful warship in the German Navy; the British Admiralty assumed that she was the most powerful warship in the world. She was constructed by Blohm and Voss of Hamburg and on St Valentine's Day 1939, went down the slipway to the acclaim of Hitler, Raeder, Keitel, Goering, Goebbels, Hess, Ribbentrop, Himmler, Bormann and von Schirach, all of whom were on the podium. At the appointed moment, Bismarck's granddaughter, Dorothea von

Loewenfeld, christened their greatest ship with the name of Germany's greatest Chancellor. The *Bismarck* 'symbolised not only a resurgent Navy but the whole resurgent German nation'.[83]

The *Bismarck*'s main armament were her eight 15-inch guns mounted on two forward turrets and two after turrets. Her excellent Zeiss stereoscopic range-finders were superior to the British co-incidences range-finders. She had a length of 791 feet and a beam of 118 feet and her displacement was listed at 35,000 tons. Her actual displacement was 42,000 tons and over 50,000 tons fully laden. Royal Navy Intelligence knew little about the *Bismarck*'s armour. The 1940 edition of *Jane's fighting Ships* cryptically described the armour of the *Bismarck* as 'not reported'.[84] In fact, the *Bismarck* had 'thirteen-inch armour made of specially hardened Wotan steel on her turrets and sides'.[85] Her deck armour was thicker than the deck armour of the largest British man-of-war, HMS *Hood*. The *Bismarck*'s total complement was 1,200. Her mission was to break out into the Atlantic with her consort, *Prinz Eugen*, and attack British convoys. The individual with the ultimate responsibility for success or failure was Admiral Lütjens. He was described as 'a man wholly dedicated to the service, courageous, single-minded, stoical, austere, taciturn as a Cistercian monk'.[86] The *Bismarck*'s captain, Ernst Lindemann, aged 45, was 'clever and cool, top of the term as a cadet, specialist in gunnery, chain smoker, and coffee-drinker, blond hair sleeked back'.[87]

The man who would soon become Lütjens' nemesis was Commander-in-Chief of the Home Fleet, Admiral Sir John C. Tovey, then aged 56. He was 'a small, blue-eyed, twinkly man, last of a family of eleven. He entered the Navy at fifteen, won his spurs at Jutland commanding the destroyer *Onslow*, helped sink the German light cruiser *Wiesbaden*, at one moment in the battle was quite close to Raeder … He was a natural leader, radiated confidence and could be quite fierce sometimes but it soon passed.'[88] A jokey Admiral wrote of him when captain of HMS *Rodney*, 'Captain Tovey shares one characteristic with me. In myself I would call it tenacity of purpose. In Tovey I can only call it sheer bloody obstinacy.'[89]

In the forenoon of 21 May Spitfires of the Coastal Command Photographic Reconnaissance Unit made a sweep of the Norwegian coast from Oslo Fjord to as far north as Bergen. One of the pilots sighted two warships in the secluded Grimstad Fjord just south of Bergen, which he photographed. Within two hours experts positively identified the larger warship as the *Bismarck*.

Admiral Tovey received this information between 1500 and 1630. He was certain that neither of the German warships would remain in Bergen waters where they were well within the range of the RAF. For the German squadron to break out into the Atlantic, it had to traverse one of four passages, the Denmark Strait between Iceland and Greenland, the passage between Iceland and the Faroes, the passage between the Faroes and the Shetlands, or the passage between the Shetlands and the Orkneys. Tovey and his staff concluded that the Denmark Strait was the most likely choice.

At some point on 21 May the Commander-in-Chief made his initial disposition of the Home Fleet. He sent the heavy cruiser *Suffolk* to join *Norfolk*, also a heavy cruiser, in the Denmark Strait. He put Vice Admiral L.E. Holland in command of a squadron consisting of Admiral Holland's flagship, the battle cruiser *Hood*, and Captain Leach's *Prince of Wales* and six destroyers on two hours' notice to be ready to steam to a position south of Iceland to cover both the Denmark Strait and the Iceland-Faroes passage. Tovey's flagship *King George V*, at the time the only sister ship to *Prince of Wales*, would remain at Scapa Flow to cover the passages south of the Faroes. *King George V* would soon be joined by the battle cruiser *Repulse*.

For Admiral Tovey, Admiral Holland and Captain Leach the afternoon of Wednesday 21 May was filled with feverish activity and great anticipation. The prospect that the decisive naval engagement of the war was about to take place was never out of their thoughts. Leach tried to put those concerns out of his mind. He could have used six additional months for working up his new battleship, but he did not have that luxury. Workmen from Vickers-Armstrongs were still aboard *Prince of Wales* correcting problems with her 14-inch guns when she went into battle.

Shortly before 1800 on 21 May Captain Leach likely visited the flagship to confer with Admiral Holland who would be in command of both *Hood* and *Prince of Wales* during any engagement with the *Bismarck*. Holland, aged 54, a gunnery specialist, was slim and short with almost totally white hair. He openly aspired to be First Sea Lord. One of his contemporaries, perhaps with a tinge of sarcasm, referred to him as 'that very clever, cool headed Lancelot Holland'.[90] In the supreme moment of his career he would prove to be far too sure of himself, but Holland certainly knew that the 21-year-old *Hood* had a potentially fatal flaw:

her deck armour was no more than three inches thick. His plan was to destroy the *Bismarck* early in the battle before she could fire a shell and breach the armour. It is conceivable that this tactic might have worked because with his eight 15-inch guns and Captain Leach's ten 14-inch guns, his squadron had eighteen heavy guns to Admiral Lütjens' eight. Holland had one other advantage; *Hood* was the fastest battle cruiser in the world with a speed of 31 knots, making her faster than the *Bismarck*.

Holland informed Leach that he wanted to maintain tight control over *Prince of Wales*. Her position would be astern of *Hood* and she would conform her movements to the latter's. She would only fire her heavy guns on Admiral Holland's order and Leach had to defer to the Admiral's commands.

In the early evening of 21 May Captain Leach was – in stereotypical British fashion – both understated and undaunted. He mustered the ship's company on the quarterdeck. Speaking from the top of the turret, he 'told them what he'd told Tovey, thanked them for their hard work during exercises and hoped they'd acquit themselves well if and when battle came.'[91]

Around 2100, Tovey acted decisively. He did not then know whether the *Bismarck* and her consort had left Bergen, but if they had and if they were heading at high speed for the Denmark Strait, he knew that he had to reinforce his two cruisers that he had already dispatched. He signalled Admiral Holland to proceed to his station south of Iceland. Before midnight, *Hood*, *Prince of Wales* and their six destroyers vanished into the Atlantic. None on shore would ever see *Hood* again.

In the Denmark Strait the pack ice extended 100 miles or more from the coast of Greenland towards Iceland. On Friday 23 May, above the ice and for approximately three miles south-easterly, the sky was clear and the ice fields shimmered in the sunshine. Over the rest of the strait heavy fog and mist extended almost to the coast of Iceland. Most of the German sailors had never been out of the Baltic and were amazed by the stark beauty of the vast pack ice of the northern seas. Many of the British sailors had been on patrol for days and had grown accustomed to their arctic environment.

Around 1900, Captain R.M. Ellis in *Suffolk* was hugging the edge of the mist on a south-westerly course. He was being deliberately cautious so that if he suddenly encountered the enemy, he could quickly disappear into the mists. His job was to send out a signal that the enemy was in sight and then to shadow them. He could not possibly engage the *Bismarck*. Ellis had ordered extra lookouts because his recently installed radar was blind astern of his ship and his view from the compass platform was obstructed. At 1922 the after look-out, Able Seaman Newell, cried out 'Ship bearing Green 140 [degrees], quickly corrected to "two ships" on the same bearing.'[92] Captain Ellis took a look through his binoculars and saw that it was the *Bismarck* and *Prinz Eugen*.

Within minutes *Suffolk* sent out the signal that the enemy had been sighted but for unknown reasons neither the Admiralty nor the Commander-in-Chief of the Home Fleet received it. The only other Royal Navy ship patrolling the Denmark Strait that night was HMS *Norfolk*. *Norfolk* was the flagship of this small squadron under the command of Rear Admiral W.F. Wake-Walker. At 2030 *Norfolk* suddenly came out of thick mist to sight the *Bismarck* and the *Prinz Eugen* off her port bow. The range was less than six miles and closing. The *Bismarck* commenced frighteningly accurate fire with her forward turrets; three salvos straddled *Norfolk* and another came down in her wake, but the latter narrowly escaped into the mists. *Norfolk*'s signal that it had received fire from the *Bismarck* was the first information that the Admiralty and the Commander-in-Chief, Admiral Tovey, received of the *Bismarck*'s exact location.

The Royal Navy now closed in for the kill. The nearest heavy units were *Hood* and *Prince of Wales*. Admiral Holland had picked up the signal from *Suffolk* a few minutes after 2030 at which point the *Bismarck* was plotted about 300 miles distant nearly due north (005 degrees). Soon after learning the location of the *Bismarck* Captain Leach spoke over his ship's loudspeaker to inform the ship's company that they should be within range of the enemy early tomorrow. The weather had deteriorated badly. Intermittent haze, fog, rain and later, snow squalls, combined to make visibility poor. Heavy seas prevented the destroyers from keeping up and they gradually fell astern.

Unaccountably, Holland decided that action with the *Bismarck* could take place any time after 0140. The Vice Admiral, therefore, ordered both *Hood* and *Prince of Wales* to action stations at 0015. Each ship hoisted her largest white ensign and the eight 15-inch guns in *Hood* and the ten 14-inch guns in *Prince of Wales* were made ready for instant use. Men not on watch were told that they could sleep at their action stations.

As *Prince of Wales* steamed several hundred yards astern of *Hood*, Captain Leach got no rest, remaining on the bridge the whole night.

By 0400 the enemy was estimated to be only 20 miles to the northwest. Leach had prepared himself and his ship as well as he could, but he felt the need for divine intercession. He knew that many others did as well, as most of his men were very young and unaccustomed to battle. He knew that they would welcome a prayer by their padre. This story is best told in the words of H.V. Morton, who learned it first hand from a participant.

> 'We were waiting the order to fire,' said one young man. 'We knew it would come at any moment and we were ready. Then, instead of the order, we heard the Padre reading a prayer. But we got the order to fire soon after.'
>
> I had already heard that story from the chaplain, the Reverend W.G. Parker. Just before action was joined he was called to the bridge by Captain Leach.
>
> 'Padre, we are going into action,' said the Captain, 'and we shall need help. I want you to read a prayer to the ship's company. Can you remember the prayer which begins, "O, God, thou knowest how busy I am ..."?'
>
> 'Yes, sir,' replied the Padre. 'It's called 'Sir Jacob Astley's prayer before Edgehill,' and I have the words in my cabin.'
>
> 'Go then, and fetch it quickly,' said the Captain. 'There's not much time.'
>
> While the battleship, steaming into action , was taut with expectancy, every nerve stretched to meet the explosion of the fourteen-inch guns, instead of the order to fire there came to every corner of the ship, from engine room to crow's nest, the sound of the Chaplain's voice saying:
>
> 'O Lord, Thou knowest how busy we must be to-day, if we forget Thee, do not Thou forget us; for Christ's sake. Amen.'
>
> Then the guns fired.[93]

By approaching the German ships at an angle Holland made his first error. His squadron could only fire those guns that could train over the bows; thus in the opening minutes of the engagement both German ships had the advantage of firing broadsides with all sixteen of their guns. This error was quickly compounded by another. Holland misidentified the *Prinz Eugen* as the *Bismarck* and ordered both of his ships to concentrate their fire on the cruiser instead of the battleship. Finally there was Holland's insistence that *Prince of Wales* steam in tight formation with *Hood*, decreeing that she should remain a few hundred yards astern of *Hood* and engage the *Bismarck* in accordance with his orders. It would have been far better if Admiral Holland had allowed Captain Leach to operate on his own. *Hood* fired her first salvo at 0600 and the *Bismarck* and *Prinz Eugen* immediately returned fire. *Prince of Wales* opened fire seconds later.

Captain Leach and his gunnery officer, Lieutenant Commander McMullen, were sure that Admiral Holland had ordered fire on the wrong ship and from the very outset Leach ordered *Prince of Wales* to fire only at the *Bismarck*. Almost immediately one of the guns in a forward turret malfunctioned and would remain useless. The after turret's four guns could not be brought to bear because of the angle of their approach to the German ships. Because the A and B turret range-finders were covered by spray, the opening fire was controlled by a relatively small range-finder in the Director Control Tower. It initially overestimated the range of the *Bismarck* by 1,000 yards.

While the fire from *Hood* and *Prince of Wales* was divided between the *Prinz Eugen* and the *Bismarck*, the German ships concentrated their guns (eight 15-inch and eight 8-inch) on the leading British ship, *Hood*. With a more rapid rate of fire and better range-finding equipment, the *Prinz Eugen* scored the first hit of the engagement striking *Hood* near her mainmast. A large fire broke out and rapidly spread forward. To watchers in *Suffolk* and *Norfolk* it resembled a big semi-circle of flame like the top half of a setting sun.

Only six minutes into the engagement, Holland ordered a Blue Pendant turn together of 20° to port. This would have opened each ship's A arc and allowed all their heavy guns to fire on the *Bismarck*. Just as the flagship began her turn away from the German ships there were two enormous splashes alongside *Hood*. Immediately afterwards a third shell plunged through *Hood*'s light deck armour and exploded near the after magazine. A huge explosion sent flames hundreds of feet into the air above *Hood*'s masts and for a few seconds her bow and stern rose into the air before disappearing under the icy waters.

Captain Leach, on the bridge of *Prince of Wales*, absorbed what happened but he was far too busy to dwell on the loss of *Hood*. His self-discipline forced him to react to the immediate danger of colliding with what little remained of the stricken vessel. *Prince of Wales* had been turning to port but now Leach ordered a hard turn to starboard, steaming her past the wreckage at high speed.

Before *Hood* blew up Captain Leach had the satisfaction of seeing one of his salvos straddle the *Bismarck*, but with the destruction of *Hood* Admiral Lütjens directed the fire of both the *Bismarck* and *Prinz Eugen* at the *Prince of Wales*. Thus far she had escaped any damage. The range between the *Bismarck* and *Prince of Wales* was now only 18,000 yards and *Prince of Wales* was receiving fire from the *Bismarck*'s eight 15-inch guns plus six of her twelve 5.9-inch guns, and from all eight of the *Prinz Eugen*'s 8-inch guns. The rate of fire of the German ships was extremely rapid: every 20 seconds from the *Bismarck*'s heavy guns and every 10 seconds from the *Prinz Eugen*'s guns. *Prince of Wales*' view toward the enemy was soon blocked by enormous curtains of splashes that reached over the masthead and the sound of *Prince of Wales*' own guns was deafening.

At this moment in the battle *Prince of Wales*' senior officers were fortunately not all standing together on the bridge. Captain Leach was on the compass platform above the admiral's bridge and the ship's navigating officer, Lieutenant Commander Powell, stood near him. The *Prince of Wales*' executive officer, Commander Lawson, had discretion to move about the ship and it is not clear where he was, but the gunnery officer, Lieutenant Commander McMullen, was in the director control tower above and abaft the compass platform directing the fire of the ship's main armament.

In the midst of this sound and fury a 15-inch shell from the *Bismarck* struck the compass platform of *Prince of Wales*, exploding after it exited. Most on the platform, including two midshipmen, were killed. Captain Leach and the Chief Yeomen of Signals were briefly knocked unconscious. The only other survivor on the bridge was the navigating officer who was wounded. The time was 0602 and about the same time another heavy shell hit *Prince of Wales*' hull aft and let in 400 tons of water.

Miraculously, Leach was able to carry on, but the compass platform was a shambles so he quickly descended to the admiral's bridge. The range of the enemy ships was now down to 14,500 yards and *Prince of Wales* was almost within range of the *Prinz Eugen*'s torpedoes. Leach now faced a critical decision, the most critical of his naval career. With no time to analyse or consult, the decision rested on him alone. He had to decide whether he should break off the engagement, and he decided that if he continued he would needlessly lose his ship and most of his men. He ordered a turn of 160° to port behind a smoke screen. This decision demonstrated Leach's ability to think clearly in the heat of battle; it was his finest hour.

In twenty minutes, *Prince of Wales* had lost two officers and eleven men killed, one officer and eight men wounded. The ship had received seven hits – four 15-inch shells and three 8-inch shells. Besides the damage to the compass platform, the communications to the steering wheel had been destroyed. The director to the forward 5.5-inch guns had been put out of action and the ship's aircraft crane had been ruined along with the ship's aircraft. After returning to harbour it was discovered that yet another heavy shell had pierced the hull deep under water and had passed through several protecting bulkheads, coming to rest without exploding.

This damage was not, however, the crucial factor in Captain Leach's decision to break off the engagement. Rather it was the mechanical defects that were developing almost continually with his guns despite the best efforts of the Vickers-Armstrongs technicians in the turrets, thus giving him no chance to destroy the *Bismarck*. Yet another problem arose just as *Prince of Wales* veered away from the German vessel. The shell ring in Y turret jammed and rendered the four guns in that turret inoperable.

With Admiral Holland's death Rear Admiral Wake-Walker in *Norfolk* became the senior officer of the squadron. He chose to shadow the two German ships until the Commander-in-Chief, Admiral Sir John Tovey, flying his flag in *King George V*, and the battle cruiser, *Repulse*, could join the battle, which promised the certain destruction of the *Bismarck*. For ten hours Wake-Walker's three ships shadowed the enemy in deteriorating weather. Just before 1600 on 24 May Wake-Walker received a signal from the Admiralty in Whitehall 'which caused him a certain amount of perplexity and some concern.'[94] The Admiralty requested his intentions as regards *Prince of Wales* re-engaging the *Bismarck*. Every officer in the Royal Navy 'is particularly sensitive to even the faintest suggestion that his ardour for battle may be in any degree lacking.'[95] There is little doubt that this was what the Admiralty was suggesting as it came from the First Sea Lord, Sir Dudley Pound, whose reputation for 'back seat driving' was notorious. Wake-Walker allowed himself some time to compose his thoughts. In due course, he replied that *Prince of Wales* should not re-engage until other heavy ships were in contact or unless interception failed. He added that it was 'doubtful whether the *Prince of Wales* had enough speed to compel an action.'[96] Sir Dudley made no attempt to overrule Wake-Walker, but after the battle the First Sea Lord tried to turn this into a court martial offence against both Wake-Walker and Leach.

At 1830 the unexpected happened. The *Bismarck* being about 26,000 yards ahead of *Suffolk* first disappeared in a fog bank then reappeared within minutes at a range of 22,000 yards firing her forward guns at the British ship. Captain Leach, then between *Suffolk* and *Norfolk*, returned the fire at very long range, about 30,000 yards. Neither side scored a hit although *Prince of Wales* was able to fire twelve salvos before two of her guns again went out of action. By 1900 the *Bismarck* had turned away from the British squadron.

In this northern latitude in late May it remained light until midnight. Captain Leach had no way of knowing whether in the fading light the *Bismarck* might alter her course by 180° and re-engage. The *Prince of Wales*'s Y turret was permanently out of action, at least three guns in A and B turrets had previously malfunctioned and would almost certainly malfunction again. *Prince of Wales*' captain was not despondent, but he knew that the odds were not in his favour in a one-on-one battle with the *Bismarck*.

On the bridge of the *Bismarck* Admiral Lütjens reassessed his own perilous situation. He had engaged *Suffolk* not to start a final battle with the British squadron but rather to mask the withdrawal of the *Prinz Eugen*, which, at high speed, had slipped away to the southwest. Admiral Lütjens, Captain Lindemann and every other officer in the *Bismarck* and indeed the entire ship's company knew that unless they could shake off the three British ships, on the morrow they could expect to encounter most of the British Home Fleet. The hours of darkness on the night of 24/25 May would be Lütjens's final opportunity to escape certain destruction.

That night in *Suffolk*, *Norfolk* and *Prince of Wales* there was little rest for the weary British sailors and none for Admiral Wake-Walker and Captain Leach who stayed on their bridges. They did their utmost to stay alert; Wake-Walker used Benzedrine and strong coffee. Unknown to many, Captain Leach had received an internal injury when the 15-inch shell struck the compass platform, and he was suffering from this and extreme fatigue. The radar operators in *Suffolk* were also desperately tired, but they had no choice but to continue tracking the *Bismarck* whenever she could not be sighted. Theirs was the only operating radar set in any of the British ships.

Before the day ended Admiral Lütjens was confronted with nine ancient Swordfish biplanes, each carrying an 18-inch torpedo slung under its belly. According to British historian Ludovic Kennedy the Swordfish, 'looked like survivors of Richthofen's Circus, cruising speed 95mph and that was pushing it.'[97] Unknown to Lütjens, *King George V*, *Repulse*, and the aircraft carrier *Victorious* were only 100 miles to the east and closing.

Shortly before midnight the Swordfish attacked. The only torpedo to hit the *Bismarck* caused little damage. An hour after this the *Bismarck* and *Prince of Wales* briefly exchanged fire for the last time but there were no hits on either ship.

Some time in the early hours of 25 May, Admiral Wake-Walker received a signal indicating that German U-boats could be encountered. He ordered his squadron to implement zigzagging. The three British ships were now trailing the *Bismarck* in a close formation with *Suffolk* in the lead, *Norfolk* in the centre and *Prince of Wales* astern. All the British ships were stationed on the port side of the *Bismarck*. Because darkness and intermittent fog obscured the German vessel, Wake-Walker had to depend entirely on *Suffolk*'s radar to locate his adversary. Fortunately for Lütjens, when *Suffolk* zigzagged to port away from the *Bismarck* she temporarily lost radar contact. She only regained contact fifteen minutes after she had turned back to starboard.

Around 0300 Admiral Lütjens and his navigating officer learned that the British ships were all on the port side of their wake. They may have also guessed that *Suffolk* temporarily lost radar contact with the *Bismarck*. Shortly after 0300 Captain Lindemann ordered the helmsmen to put the wheel to starboard. Slowly the *Bismarck* made a huge loop, a move unknown to either Wake-Walker or Leach. Three hours later the *Bismarck* crossed her own wake and that of her shadowers heading on a course of 130° which pointed her at the north-western coast of Spain. She had successfully shaken off Wake-Walker's squadron. It was then approximately 0600 Sunday 25 May and the *Bismarck* would elude the Royal Navy and RAF Coastal Command for over 24 hours.

Captain Leach's disappointment was understandable. Before the *Bismarck* vanished, he had every expectation of successfully engaging her in the forenoon of 25 May. By then his ship would have been reinforced by *King George V* and *Repulse*. Outnumbered and outgunned the *Bismarck* would have faced certain destruction, but the battle that Wake-Walker and Leach had anticipated never took place. What Leach had no way of knowing was that one of *Prince of Wales'* 14-inch shells had caused serious damage to the *Bismarck* that would contribute significantly to her demise. This shell had struck the port bow near the waterline, penetrated two oil tanks and exited the starboard side without exploding. The *Bismarck's* damage control officers and men had worked frantically to prevent more water getting in by putting down collision mats to cover the two holes in the bows but oil had continued to leak. Oil pumps and pipeline valves were out of action and the end result was that her engines were deprived of 1,000 tons of oil from the forward tanks. In order to conserve fuel the *Bismarck's* maximum speed was reduced to 28 knots and later to 20, preventing her from reaching the protective cover of the Luftwaffe. German bombers were capable of operating at longitude 14° west; the *Bismarck* was sunk in the vicinity of longitude 16° west.

After Admiral Wake-Walker realised that the *Bismarck* had vanished he decided that his two cruisers no longer needed the protection of *Prince of Wales*. She was first ordered to join *King George V*, but before that took place she was directed to Iceland for refuelling. The next day Captain Leach learned that the *Bismarck* had been sighted by a Coastal Command aircraft, and over the following 24 hours he followed every report in minute detail. The chase and ultimate destruction of the *Bismarck* captivated the British nation and has been well covered by historians, but a brief description of her demise has been included.

At 1030 on Monday 26 May, US Navy Ensign Leonard Smith, who was on loan to the Royal Air Force, was the co-pilot of Coastal Command Catalina Z209, searching for any trace of the *Bismarck*. Suddenly Smith spotted a large warship steaming eastward some eight miles away; his immediate comment to the aircraft's captain, Pilot Officer Dennis A. Briggs, was 'what the devil's that?'[98] Both stared at the black object ploughing through very rough seas. Smith said, 'Looks like a battleship.'[99] The enemy ship's anti-aircraft fire then erupted with such force that he had to take violent evasive action.

It was indeed the *Bismarck* and the Royal Navy started closing their net with ships and aircraft. It was nonetheless a close run thing. Not until 2130 did Swordfish from the carrier *Ark Royal* attack the *Bismarck*. Despite intensive anti-aircraft fire the aircraft managed two hits, one on the port side amidship, the other on the starboard side well aft, which damaged the *Bismarck's* rudders and reduced her to a helpless cripple.

She could only be steered in one direction and that brought her ever closer to the British fleet.

The next day the heavy guns of *King George V* and *Rodney* reduced the *Bismarck* to a hulk at ranges down to 2,900 yards, but still she did not sink. Finally Admiral Tovey ordered the cruiser *Dorchester* to sink her with torpedoes. The cruiser fired two torpedoes into her starboard side and one into her port. 'At 1036 with her flag still flying, she rolled over and disappeared at 48°10′N, 16°12′W taking with her Lütjens, Lindemann and all but 110 members of her company of 2,200.'[100]

Notwithstanding his relief that the *Bismarck* had been sunk and no longer posed a threat to vital convoys, the First Sea Lord Sir Dudley Pound was far from pleased by the overall results. The Royal Navy had lost *Hood*, which in the eyes of the British public and most of the English speaking world was the very symbol of British naval power. *Prince of Wales* had been roughly handled and the *Prinz Eugen* had escaped.

Sir Dudley lacked any recent experience in fleet engagements. Moreover, in May 1941, he was an ill man. He had a brain tumour which would ultimately take his life. He also suffered from a hip disease that caused pain and insomnia. Nevertheless, Pound's efforts to court martial both Admiral Wake-Walker and Captain Leach were reprehensible. He proposed to Admiral Tovey that Wake-Walker and Leach be tried for Leach's decision to disengage from his battle with the *Bismarck* and for Wake-Walker's decision to shadow the *Bismarck* rather than re-engage. Tovey was utterly appalled and informed the First Sea Lord that the last thing he wanted was a premature action and commended both Wake-Walker and Leach for their conduct throughout the engagement. Without reflection, Pound declared that if Tovey would not order the court martial, the Admiralty would. Tovey then showed his character and his personal regard for both Wake-Walker and Leach. He bluntly told the First Sea Lord that if the Admiralty proceeded with their courts martial, he would strike his flag as Commander-in-Chief and appear at the trial as prisoner's friend. 'After that,' said Tovey, 'I heard no more about it.'[101]

In late May *Prince of Wales* proceeded to Rosyth for the repair of the damage inflicted by the *Bismarck* and entered a dry dock. That night Captain Leach retired to his quarters on the main deck just below the quarterdeck. He undoubtedly hoped to enjoy a good night's rest. His ship was as well protected from bombs, shells and torpedoes as she could possibly be and it seemed that only a direct hit by a bomber could pose a threat. What he did not know was that there was an unexploded 15-inch shell from the *Bismarck* in the bottom of the ship. Some time between 0000 and 0400 the officer of the watch, Sub Lieutenant Geoffrey Brooke, sprinted from the quarterdeck lobby to alert the captain to this newly discovered danger. While Brooke did not display panic, the young officer was clearly alarmed. Brooke later wrote of 'feeling very relieved that the galaxy of talent that tumbled down the hatchways, buttoning coats over pyjamas as it went, was between me and the awkward decisions that would have to be made.'[102] The 2000lb shell was removed from *Prince of Wales* with some difficulty by cutting a hole in her hull. Whether Captain Leach ever caught up on his sleep that night seems doubtful.

When he became sovereign, King George VI still identified with the Royal Navy. On the first night of his reign, he told his cousin Lord Louis Mountbatten, 'Dickie, this is absolutely terrible; I never wanted this to happen; I am quite unprepared for it. I've never even seen a State Paper. I'm only a Naval Officer. It's the only thing I know about.'[103] The King followed the battle in the Denmark Strait and the subsequent pursuit and destruction of the *Bismarck* with enormous interest. His diaries reveal that he not only had a full appreciation for the tactics and strategy involved, but had manifest sympathy for Leach's decisions in the heat of battle. The reader should bear in mind that at the time the King was not aware of the extent to which the main armament of *Prince of Wales* had repeatedly malfunctioned and that Leach had no chance of destroying the *Bismarck*.

27 May
... The Prime Minister came to lunch. He was delighted with the sinking of the 'Bismarck' as it makes our Atlantic position better, in that we have only the 'Tirpitz' to deal with now. The 'B' & 'T' are the only German modern battleships. We shall have three very soon, the 'K.G.V.,' the 'P of W,' and the 'D of Y' with which to take on the 'Tirpitz.' The 'Bismarck' was certainly unsinkable by gunfire ...[104]

4 June
... I saw R. Adl Syfret (late Naval Secy) as he is going to sea. Such a nice man, & kept me well informed from the Admiralty. He told me details of the action against the 'Bismarck.' Capt. John Leach of the 'P of W' is criticised for breaking off the action with 'B' after 'Hood' was sunk. His ship had been hit on the bridge & the fire control damaged. Also 'Y' turret

was out of action (4 guns). Out of 14 people on the bridge, 11 were killed or wounded. No wonder Leach wanted time to think!! ...[105]

On 16 June Captain Leach was admitted to Bovey Tracey District Hospital for hernia surgery, a more serious operation in 1941 than it is today. He was not discharged until 25 June and he went to Yarner on sick leave. He and his wife had much to celebrate and this time of recovery was his longest stay at Yarner during the war.

Leach returned to *Prince of Wales* at Scapa Flow on 1 August. The reception that he received is best told in the words of Sub Lieutenant Brooke.

Just before leaving Rosyth the Captain went to hospital for a hernia operation. He was relieved for a short time by Captain C.H. Harcourt who took us back to the Flow ...

There was, of course, nothing untoward about our temporary CO, in fact he shortly became an Admiral, but naturally he was not held in as much affection as Captain Leach. The depth of this affection was well illustrated on the latter's return. It was the middle of the forenoon when the Captain's boat was seen approaching. With a flash of inspiration the Commander – presumably after a word with the substitute skipper – went to the Bo's'n's Mate's microphone in the adjacent lobby and said, 'Captain Leach is returning to the ship. Those of you who would like to welcome him back may lay aft.' The forward end of the quarterdeck and the whole of the after superstructure overlooking it suddenly began to sprout sailors, unseen by the Captain who by now was under the lee of the stern. As he appeared at the top of the gangway the Commander took off his cap and shouted, 'Three cheers for Captain Leach!' who was taken completely by surprise. The cheers rang out from a solid mass of men and heaven knows what the other ships thought was going on. It was all very irregular but most satisfactory. The Captain stood astonished for a second, then waved his hand and went down to his cabin with his stand-in. He passed close to me and I saw that tears were glistening on his cheeks.[106]

The Admiralty did not lightly bestow decorations during the Second World War but on 14 October 1941 the *London Gazette* informed its readers that Captain J.C. Leach MVO had been awarded DSO (Companion of the Distinguished Service Order) for mastery, determination and skill in action against the German battleship *Bismarck*.

Yarner – From 1916 to 1941, Yarner was the home of Captain and Mrs John C. Leach. It is situated one mile west of Bovey Tracey in Devon. Yarner is a Grade II listed seventeenth-century building, but its origins are much older. It appears in the Patent Rolls of 1344 as Yarnour/Yarnouere. *(Courtesy of Admiral of the Fleet Sir Henry Leach GCB DL)*

Cadet Leach with his team mates from the Dartmouth cricket team, *c.*1910. He is on the far left of the photograph. *(Courtesy of the Britannia Museum at Britannia Royal Naval College Dartmouth)*

Captain Leach's wife Evelyn with their two sons, Roger and Henry, at Yarner, *c.*1929. *(Courtesy of Admiral of the Fleet Sir Henry Leach GCB DL)*

A bomb blast off the stern of USS *Augusta* on 14 August 1937. This photograph was taken from HMS *Cumberland*, then commanded by Captain Leach. *(Courtesy of Admiral of the Fleet Sir Henry Leach GCB DL)*

Captain Leach with HMS *Cumberland*'s soccer team and four of the ship's officers, *c.*1937. *(Courtesy of Admiral of the Fleet Sir Henry Leach GCB DL)*

The launching of HMS *Prince of Wales* at the Cammell Laird Yard in Birkenhead on 3 May 1939. HMS *Prince of Wales* was christened by Mary, the Princess Royal, the younger sister of King George VI and godmother to his elder daughter, HM Queen Elizabeth II. *(Courtesy of The Times Archives)*

King George VI's inspection of his newest battleship, HMS *Prince of Wales*, on 6 March 1941. Captain Leach is slightly behind and on the King's right. This occasion marked the first contact since the Royal Tour in HMS *Renown* in 1927. *(Courtesy of Imperial War Museum)*

King George VI's inspection of sailors in HMS *Prince of Wales* on 6 March 1941. Captain Leach is the tall officer bending over on the left side of the photograph. *(Courtesy of Imperial War Museum)*

King George VI with officers from the Royal Navy, the British Army and the Royal Air Force at Pitreavie Castle near Rosyth. Captain Leach is standing behind King George VI and Admiral Bertram Ramsay, early April 1941. *(Courtesy of Admiral of the Fleet Sir Henry Leach GCB DL)*

Sketch made by Captain Leach of the explosion that destroyed HMS *Hood* following a hit by a 15-inch shell from the *Bismarck*. At the time his ship, HMS *Prince of Wales*, was at a distance of four cables. *(Courtesy of Churchill College, Cambridge University)*

Able Seaman Newell, lookout on HMS *Suffolk*. He was the first man to spot the *Bismark* in the Denmark Strait. *(Royal Naval Museum)*

Admiral Sir John Tovey, Commander in Chief of Home Fleet, and Captain Leach near Y turret in HMS *Prince of Wales* not long after the action with the *Bismarck*. *(Courtesy of Admiral of the Fleet Sir Henry Leach GCB DL)*

Prime Minister Churchill speaking to Admiral Sir Dudley Pound and Captain Leach on Saturday 9 August 1941, the day that HMS *Prince of Wales* arrived at Placentia Bay Newfoundland for the first summit meeting between Churchill and Roosevelt. Mr Harry L. Hopkins, Roosevelt's closest adviser, is standing behind Churchill. *(Courtesy of Imperial War Museum)*

Captain Leach on the quarterdeck of HMS *Prince of Wales*. There is a telescope under Captain Leach's left arm. This was not simply a 'prop' for the camera. In 1941 radar could not distinguish a hostile ship from a friendly ship. A telescope, therefore, could actually be very useful to a ship's captain. *(Courtesy of Imperial War Museum)*

Captain Leach's welcome to President Franklin D. Roosevelt on Sunday morning, 10 August 1941. The ship's captain always greets any distinguished visitor at the gangway. *(Courtesy of Imperial War Museum)*

Captain Leach greets the president's son, Captain Elliott Roosevelt, United States Army Air Corps. *(Courtesy of Imperial War Museum)*

The most famous church parade of the Second World War. Captain Leach is standing behind and slightly to the right of the chaplain at the lectern. The two persons seated are President Roosevelt and Prime Minister Churchill. Behind them in the first row are, left to right, Air Chief Marshal Sir Wilfred R. Freeman, Admiral Ernest J. King, General George C. Marshall, Lieutenant General Sir John G. Dill, Admiral Harold R. Stark, and Admiral Sir Dudley Pound. Behind and to the left of Dill stands Brigadier General Edwin M. Watson, a military aide and close confidant of the President, who always addressed Watson by his nickname, 'Pa'. In 1958, General Watson's widow, Frances, gave a party at Kenwood in honour of Julia Harrison Ryan, to whom this book is dedicated. *(Courtesy of the Franklin D. Roosevelt Library)*

Captain Leach is shown at his roll top desk in HMS *Prince of Wales* some time in 1941. *(Courtesy of Admiral of the Fleet Sir Henry Leach GCB DL)*

An oil painting of HMS *Prince of Wales* in action with *Bismarck* and *Prinz Eugen*. The smoke and flames in the background come from the explosion that destroyed HMS *Hood*. This painting, entitled 'The Bismarck Action: Destruction of HMS Hood' was by the famous war artist John Hamilton who spent seven years creating 84 paintings on the war at sea. *(Held in the Imperial War Museum Collection, reproduced courtesy of the John Hamilton Estate)*

The USS *Arizona* burns after the attack on Pearl Harbor, 7 December 1941. *(Courtesy of US National Archives Collection)*

HMS *Prince of Wales* illustrated in the *Gibraltar Chronicle*, 11 December 1941.

The Mitsubishi G3M Type 96 'Nell', of which 60 took part in the attack that sank HMS *Prince of Wales* and *Repulse*. This was the type's greatest success. Japan's main land-based torpedo and high level bomber pre-war, it was phased out in favour of the G4M 'Betty' from the end of 1941. (*Cody Images*)

Captain John C. Leach Royal Navy who was held in high esteem by many including King George VI and Prime Minister Churchill. *(Courtesy of Admiral of the Fleet Sir Henry Leach GCB DL)*

Chapter IX

A Voyage of Hope

There was delicious irony in the selection of Captain Leach to take Prime Minister Churchill and his entourage across the Atlantic for Churchill's first summit meeting with President Roosevelt. The senior naval officer on that historic voyage was Admiral of the Fleet Sir Dudley Pound, the First Sea Lord. There is no evidence that either Pound or Leach ever spoke of the former's attempt to court martial the latter less than three months previously.

The other two senior officers on board were Lieutenant General Sir John Dill, Chief of the Imperial General Staff and Air Marshal Sir Wilfred R. Freeman, Vice-Chief of the Air Staff. Other officers in the entourage included Colonel Leslie Hollis, senior assistant to General 'Pug' Ismay, Churchill's Chief of Staff and Lieutenant Colonel Ian Jacob, the other principal senior assistant to Ismay and Captain Richard Pim, RN. Captain Pim was in charge of Churchill's war room at the Admiralty where maps showed the positions of convoys and warships on the oceans of the world. Some at the Admiralty referred to it as 'Pim's sacred domain'[107] and he set up a replica war room in the *Prince of Wales*.

Not all of the important personages aboard *Prince of Wales* were military officers. The civilians included Sir Alexander Cadogan, permanent undersecretary of the Foreign Office, Professor Frederick Lindemann, known to Churchill as 'the Prof' who 'was Churchill's interpreter on all technical matters whether scientific or economic'[108] and John Martin, one of Churchill's private secretaries.

One bright day on this historic voyage Churchill and entourage posed for an official photograph on the quarterdeck of *Prince of Wales*. Churchill is wearing a yachting cap and blue nautical jacket with brass buttons, the uniform of the Royal Yacht Squadron. In his right hand is an unlit cigar. In addition to the aforesaid a few others were selected to be in this photograph, one of whom was Captain Leach.

Prince of Wales' passenger roster included the American Harry Lloyd Hopkins (see Chapter VI), President Roosevelt's closest adviser and an invaluable liaison between Roosevelt and Churchill. Shortly before he embarked on *Prince of Wales* Hopkins had been with Marshal Stalin in Moscow. On 22 June Germany had invaded the Soviet Union in the most massive invasion in history but despite the extent of the German advance Stalin had convinced Hopkins that Russia was not about to collapse. Hopkins was only 50, but he was an ill man living on borrowed time. Flight Lieutenant D.C. McKinley had been hand-picked to fly Hopkins to Russia and they had travelled in an American-made PBY, which the British called the Catalina, from Invergordon on the east coast of Scotland to Archangel in Russia. On their return flight they flew directly to Scapa Flow so that Hopkins could join Churchill in *Prince of Wales*. It was a gruelling flight of over 2,000 miles. Hopkins, who had left his medical kit in Moscow, suffered from exhaustion and illness, but during their short time together McKinley had grown fond of his American charge. McKinley recounted his last view of Hopkins after he had landed his aircraft on the choppy water of the Flow.

At this stage Mr Hopkins had to make a hazardous leap from the aircraft to the launch followed by his luggage which was literally hurled across the several yards of open water separating us from the launch. My last glimpse of him showed him smiling and determined, though very dishevelled as the result of his wearing experience. As he waved us farewell we could not help feeling that very few persons could have taken what he had endured since we met at Invergordon on July 28. Circling overhead prior to our return flight to Oban we saw a launch wallowing heavily across the harbour and we wondered if there was to be any rest for a man so obviously ill and yet showing unbelievable courage, determination and appreciation for the services of others.[109]

That launch deposited Hopkins at the *Prince of Wales*. It was still over 24 hours before *Prince of Wales* was scheduled to depart and Churchill was not yet aboard. That night the Commander-in-Chief Admiral Tovey and Captain Leach hosted a dinner for Hopkins, but he was too ill to enjoy his food and Admiral Tovey immediately summoned medical assistance. The American was medicated and put to bed where he slept until the following afternoon.

Captain Leach was responsible for the safety of his ship and her company. Now he had the additional responsibility for his Prime Minister, the First Sea Lord, the Chief of the Imperial General Staff, the Vice-Chief of the Air Staff, the Permanent Undersecretary of the Foreign Office, the Prime Minister's chief scientific adviser and the closest adviser to the President of the United States. The repercussions if the *Prince of Wales* had been attacked by U-boats, long range bombers or the *Tirpitz*, the sister ship of the *Bismarck*, would have been great indeed.

In the period before Britain entered the war on 3 September 1939, the defences of Scapa Flow had been badly neglected. Prime Minister Neville Chamberlain, who put too much effort into the appeasement

Libertymen leaving HMS *Royal Oak* the day before the attack by U-47.

The triumphant crew of U-47. *(Courtesy of Korvetten-Kapitan Hans Wessels)*

of Hitler, was partially to blame. At 0130 on 14 October 1939 U-47 entered Scapa Flow through a channel that was not properly guarded, and after dark located the battleship *Royal Oak*. The U-boat commander, Lieutenant Günther Prien, fired two salvos of torpedoes into the *Royal Oak* five minutes apart. Within minutes the *Royal Oak* capsized with a loss of 833 officers and ratings.

Three days later long-range bombers flying from airfields inside Germany raided Scapa Flow, damaging the former battleship *Iron Duke*, which had to be beached. These two attacks prompted the Admiralty to take immediate action. The Home Fleet was redeployed to bases on the west coast of Scotland and the Home Fleet did not return to Scapa Flow until March 1940. Counter-measures were taken to make certain that U-boats could never penetrate the Flow again, including the reinforcement of booms, additional blockships and controlled minefields. 88 heavy and 40 light anti-aircraft guns were mounted on Hoy and nearby islands, together with over 100 searchlights. On 3 January 1940 Churchill, then First Lord of the Admiralty, sent a minute to First Sea Lord Sir Dudley Pound that questioned the number of searchlights to be installed at Scapa.

> Is it really necessary to have 108 anti-aircraft lights? Is it likely that an enemy making an attack upon the Fleet at this great distance would do it by night? All their attacks up to the present have been by day, and it is only by day that precise targets can be hit.[110]

As *Prince of Wales* steamed out into the Atlantic, Leach's biggest concern was not the risk of a night bombing raid, but the possibility that a German reconnaissance aircraft would spot the ship leaving the Flow and signal a U-boat on station nearby. There was little that Leach could do about that threat except to depend on his destroyers to detect and destroy any submarines. Unbeknownst to Leach, crypto-analysts at the highly secret intelligence centre at Bletchley Park, a Victorian mansion situated 50 miles north-west of London, were daily decrypting the German naval Enigma signals which included all patrol orders to U-boats. Based on this information *Prince of Wales* was diverted from areas where U-boats were known to be operating. The threat of the *Tirpitz* intercepting *Prince of Wales* was more apparent than real. After the loss of the *Bismarck*, Hitler ordered Admiral Erich Raeder to limit the *Tirpitz*'s operations to the Baltic and Norwegian waters where she could be protected by fighter aircraft.

Churchill's long-time adviser and intimate friend Brendan Bracken, then Minister of Information, had invited two prominent authors to accompany Churchill to his historic rendezvous with Roosevelt. Henry Vollam Morton was a travel writer whose books included *The Heart of London, In Search of Scotland*, and *In the Steps of the Master*. Howard Spring was a Welsh novelist whose bestseller was *Oh, Absalom*. Shortly before 11.30 on Sunday 3 August, Morton and Spring boarded a train at Marylebone Station in London. Neither knew where he was being taken, but when they were assigned to a sleeper car they knew they were headed for Scotland. After lunch Morton noticed that the train was slowing down, and at a small country station he watched through a window as Churchill and his entourage came aboard. He heard someone call this name. It was Brendan Bracken, hatless, his auburn hair ruffled, his face beaming with delight. "'Well, you see who's on the train?" he asked eagerly. The train began to move. "Good luck!" he said as he leaped down on the platform.'[111]

Later in the afternoon Morton was talking to Spring in their day coach when Colonel Hollis joined them. He had been authorised by the Prime Minister's secretary, John Martin, to tell them they were going to Newfoundland in *Prince of Wales* where Churchill would meet the President of the United States. They wanted to know how close a secret it was. "'The best kept secret I can remember in Whitehall," he replied.'[112] They asked about the attitude of their Prime Minister. "'Well, you see," replied the Colonel, "He's rather like a boy who's been let out of school suddenly. He says it's the only holiday he's had since the war.""[113]

Shortly after breakfast the next morning the train arrived in Thurso, the closest port to Scapa Flow. Morton and Spring were taken by a drifter called *Smiling Morn* to the destroyer *Oribi* anchored in the bay. From the deck they watched Churchill and the Chiefs of Staff board. 'The mist had settled into a firm drizzle and the Prime Minister was offered shelter. "No," he said, "the bridge.""[114]

Captain Leach had planned a meticulous welcome for the dignitaries. Morton's words describe the scene.

We saw a giant among giants, the splendid ship that was to be our home, her great guns pointing fore and aft, her crew drawn up on deck. How beautiful she looked that morning as she appeared out of the mist, full of power, strength and pride. As we approached her, bells rang in our engine room, we slowed and, tilting slightly against the sea, swung around to her and, as we did so, we saw that the battleship, which from a distance had looked so graceful and so lithe, now towered above us like a mighty hill of steel. Far above us the fifteen hundred odd members of her crew stood mustered on the decks, the bosuns stood at the gangway, the Officer of the Watch with his telescope, the Captain, the Royal Marines and their band upon the quarter-deck; and it was interesting to watch the expression of the Prince of Wales as we came alongside, for every pair of eyes was upon the bridge of the Oribi, where a man was smoking a cigar; and you see lips forming words and almost hear a whisper go right around the battleship – 'It's Winston!'

He crossed the gangway from ship to ship and as his foot touched the quarter-deck he saluted and then shook hands with Captain Leach – a tall, elegant figure with a telescope tucked beneath his arm.[115]

A young officer, Lieutenant Dyer-Smith had vacated his cabin so that Morton could occupy it. When Morton apologised for this inconvenience, Dyer-Smith brushed it aside telling Morton that it was a great privilege to be taking the Prime Minister to sea and that they were all tremendously proud to have been selected. The cabin would have suited Morton perfectly except that it was directly over the propeller shaft. The noise was thunderous and the vibrations were worse than the noise. Dyer-Smith told Morton they were doing a good 30 knots and that it was not always so bad; he thought Morton would get used to it.

Captain Leach gave up his quarters to the Prime Minister, which consisted of a drawing room with chintz-covered settees and armchairs, a dining room, a bedroom, a bathroom and a pantry. Leach had for many years lived a Spartan life at sea and such luxury was not to his taste. The quarters had been designed for whichever admiral flew his flag in the *Prince of Wales* rather than a captain.

On their first night at sea, just before dinner, Leach spoke over the loudspeaker and announced that *Prince of Wales* was to carry the Prime Minister and the Chiefs of Staff to Placentia Bay, Newfoundland, to meet the President of the United States. For most of the ship's officers, Morton and Spring, dinner was served in the wardroom by Royal Marines mess attendants in white jackets. The Prime Minister, Harry Hopkins, the Chiefs of Staff and the other distinguished passengers dined in the Captain's quarters. After the tables in the wardroom were cleared, comfortable chairs were brought in from the anteroom and a screen and projector were set up. Churchill's party entered the wardroom formally attired; Sir John Dill was wearing a dinner jacket as was Harry Hopkins, Sir Dudley Pound wore his Admiral's uniform and Churchill, who was the last to enter the wardroom, wore the mess dress of the Royal Yacht Squadron. Morton saw that he was 'beaming all over and emanating a terrific good nature'.[116]

When Churchill retired for his first night in *Prince of Wales*, he could not have been in better spirits, but he soon reappeared in a petulant mood that he did not try to hide. The Captain's quarters were in the stern of the ship, and while the noise and vibrations there were not as bad as they were in Morton's cabin, they were bad enough. In the middle of the night Churchill proceeded to abandon the Captain's quarters and the first officer he encountered was ordered to escort him to the Admiral's sea cabin. This young officer thought the Prime Minister looked like an enraged cherub as they set out, Churchill wearing his famous zip up siren suit. It was not an easy journey as the *Prince of Wales* was blacked out and closed-down for instant battle and was steaming at full speed into gale force winds. Ascending and descending companion-ways in the dark the Prime Minister could have had a nasty fall, but he was able to reach his destination without mishap. Churchill found the Admiral's sea cabin much more to his liking; indeed he liked it so well that he slept there for the entire remainder of the voyage.

Churchill had always taken a special interest in the Royal Navy. He knew its history by heart and venerated Lord Nelson, the Royal Navy's greatest hero. He had also been the First Lord of the Admiralty at the outset of both world wars. On the outbound voyage to Newfoundland he read C.S. Forester's novel *Captain Horatio Hornblower RN*; it was the first book he had read for pleasure since the war began. For all this interest in the service, Churchill might not have struck up such a friendship with the Royal Navy captain of the *Prince of Wales* had he not taken the Admiral's sea cabin, which was quite near Leach's own sea cabin. Volume III of Churchill's memoirs of the Second World War, entitled *The Grand Alliance*, makes mention of the man who safeguarded him across the Atlantic.

> The spacious quarters over the propellers, which are most comfortable in harbour, became almost uninhabitable through vibration in heavy weather at sea, so I moved to the Admiral's sea cabin on the bridge for working and sleeping. I took a great liking to our Captain Leach, a charming and lovable man and all that a British sailor should be.[117]

Morton did not meet Leach until the day that *Prince of Wales* reached Placentia Bay. *Prince of Wales* with her white ensign unfurled in the morning breeze followed two American destroyers flying the Stars and Stripes into that vast bay which is 55 miles in width at its opening. Within a short time *Prince of Wales* came abreast of USS *Augusta* where the President stood on the bridge. As she did so bosun's pipes shrilled and the Royal Marines band crashed into *The Star Spangled Banner*. From *Augusta* came her response, *God Save the King*. Morton found himself in conversation with a stranger on the quarterdeck.

> While I was watching these incidents I met a strange naval officer upon the quarter-deck – a tall, elegant figure in captain's uniform, striding in

solitary state with a telescope under his arm. He had that definite air of ownership which captains assume upon their own quarter-deck. He was Captain Leach, who had been invisible from the moment of our sailing. He told me that he had been on the bridge for six days and nights, and was now properly shaved and clothed for the first time since leaving Scapa Flow. I said something about the responsibility of taking Winston Churchill across the Atlantic in war-time, and I received in reply an eloquent glance of tired blue eyes and a weary but contented smile.[118]

The next day was Sunday 10 August. Churchill and Roosevelt agreed that it was most appropriate to hold divine services, which the Royal Navy calls a 'church parade'. That morning the sun came out for the first time and Morton met Churchill on the deck. 'We have a grand day for a church parade,' he said, 'and I have chosen some grand hymns.'[119]

The American destroyer *McDougal* secured alongside the *Augusta* and took on the President, the Chiefs of Staff, Harry Hopkins, Sumner Wells, Averell Harriman and two of the President's sons. As soon as the *McDougal* was secured to *Prince of Wales* a gangway was thrown across. Franklin Roosevelt was the first American to step aboard the ship; with his left hand he held the arm of his second son, Elliott, who wore the uniform of a captain in the US Army Air Force.

Captain Leach stepped forward to welcome the President, a meeting captured in a marvellous photograph held at the Imperial War Museum. Leach is shaking the smiling President's hand. Behind Roosevelt and to his right there is a young American naval officer, the President's third son, Ensign Franklin D. Roosevelt Jr, US Navy. Churchill stands five feet away taking in everything with apparent pleasure.

Immediately thereafter the Royal Marines honour guard presented arms with rifles flashing bayonets. The Royal Marines band crashed into *The Star Spangled Banner* and the President stood at attention with his hat over his heart. His two sons saluted.

Leach read the lesson at the service, verses 5 and 6 of chapter 1 of the Book of Joshua.

There shall not any man be able to stand before thee all the days of thy life: as I was with Moses, so I will be with thee: I will not fail thee, nor forsake thee.

> Be strong and of a good courage: for unto this people shall thou divide
> for an inheritance the land, which I swore unto their fathers to give them.

On the afternoon of Tuesday 19 August, Churchill and Roosevelt concluded their conversations aboard USS *Augusta* and the Prime Minister
and his party returned in the last launch to *Prince of Wales*. At 17.00 Captain
Leach's ship passed slowly by *Augusta*, saluted the American cruiser and
steamed out of Placentia Bay. The only concrete accomplishment of
Churchill's and Roosevelt's first summit conference was the Atlantic
Charter, which is no longer in use. In a radio broadcast to the British
people on 24 August Churchill referred to it as 'a simple, rough and ready
war-time statement of the goal toward which the British Commonwealth
and the United States mean to make their way.'[120] His radio address gave
larger emphasis to the ties that had always bound Britain and the US
together rather than to the lofty, idealistic goals of the Charter.

> We had a Church Parade on the Sunday in our Atlantic bay. The President
> came on the quarter-deck of the Prince of Wales, where there were min-
> gled together many hundreds of American and British sailors and Marines.
> The sun shone bright and warm, while we sang the old hymns which
> are our common inheritance, and which we learned as children in our
> homes. We sang the hymn founded on the Psalm which John Hampden's
> soldiers sang when they bore his body to the grave, and in which the
> brief precarious span of human life is contrasted with the immutability of
> Him to whom a thousand ages are but as yesterday when it is past and as
> a watch in the night.
>
> We sang the sailor's hymn 'For those' – and there are very many – 'in
> peril on the Sea.' We sang 'Onward Christian Soldiers' and indeed, I felt
> this was no vain presumption but that we had the right to feel that we
> were serving a cause for the sake of which a trumpet had sounded from
> on high. When I looked upon that densely packed congregation of fight-
> ing men of the same language, of the same faith, of the same fundamental
> laws, of the same ideals, and now to a large extent of the same interests,
> and certainly in different degrees facing the same dangers, it swept across
> me that here was the only hope …[121]

The Atlantic Conference failed to achieve agreement over Japanese
aggression. Japan now possessed air bases within striking distance of

Singapore. These air bases were located in French Indo-China which Japan had seized in stages after the fall of France. One of Churchill's hopes at the Atlantic Conference was to convince Roosevelt that if Japan attacked either Singapore or the Netherlands East Indies, it would be in the paramount interest of the US to declare war on Japan. Churchill only managed to get Roosevelt to agree to a diplomatic note to Japan that would include the following words drafted by Churchill:

> Any further encroachment by Japan in the Southwest Pacific would produce a situation in which the United States Government would be compelled to take counter-measures, even though these might lead to war between the United States and Japan.[122]

When Roosevelt returned to Washington, his Secretary of State, Cordell Hull, strongly objected to this language. Churchill's words were deleted.

In their off-the-record discussions about the menace of Japan, Churchill and Roosevelt agreed on a show of force that they believed might lessen her militaristic ambitions. The American deterrent would be the Boeing B-17 heavy bomber, often called the Flying Fortress, with a range of 2,000 miles and a payload of 17,600lbs. There were those in the US Army Air Corps who were sure that by virtue of its speed and its armament the B-17 would seldom be shot down. These views overestimated the B-17 and underestimated the Mitsubishi A6M2 Reisen.

Roosevelt's idea for a British deterrent was a Royal Navy squadron of capital ships based at Singapore and the discussions between the two premiers may have been the reason for Churchill's decision to send HMS *Prince of Wales* and HMS *Repulse* to Singapore. On *Prince of Wales'* inbound voyage to Scapa Flow Leach had more immediate concerns than a future war with Japan. At 0730 on Wednesday 13 August he told the entire ship over the loudspeaker that the meeting between Churchill and Roosevelt had become known in Germany and that the enemy probably knew that it had taken place near Newfoundland. He went on to tell them that the danger of U-boat attack was imminent and that on the final run into Scapa the danger of air attack could not be overlooked. 'If ever there was a time when the utmost vigilance is required ... it is upon this voyage.'[123] On Monday 18 August *Prince of Wales* reached Scapa Flow after a brief stop in Iceland, having seen no sign of the enemy.

Before departing *Prince of Wales* Churchill made a farewell speech to the ship's company with whom he now felt a special bond. The officers and ratings waved their caps in the air and cheered. One of those present remembered that Churchill had smiled at the cheering sailors and brought out one of his best cigars. A destroyer was waiting with steam up to take him and his party to the Scottish mainland. As he departed he turned to bid a farewell to the *Prince of Wales*; he would never see her or her captain again.

Churchill wanted to show Leach his appreciation and in the second week of September he received a photograph of the Prime Minister together with a letter of transmittal signed by Lieutenant Commander C.R. Thompson. Thompson had been Churchill's flag lieutenant at the Admiralty and had gone to Downing Street with his master. During the war Thompson made all of Churchill's travel arrangements as well as carrying out personal assignments. The photograph was presumably lost with its owner, but Churchill's inscription is believed to have included the following words:

To Captain John C. Leach

This is a small memento of a memorable trip with my best thanks to yourself …

Winston S. Churchill

On 12 September Captain Leach sent Churchill a handwritten note.

My Dear Prime Minister

I write to thank you most gratefully for the charming photograph which arrived today and to say how delighted I am to have it.

It was indeed a memorable voyage and it will be a very long time before my sailors stop talking and writing letters about it. Nor shall we forget the honour done to the *Prince of Wales* by your visit – I was so glad that an opportunity arose for you to go to sea in one of these two ships with which you have been so much concerned.

The material continues to improve – and it will continue to do so for some time yet. But I have no doubt whatever that it is at least twice as efficient as it was when we met the *Bismarck* and I am sure that it will in the end be thoroughly satisfactory and reliable.

Thank you again so much for the Photograph. We all hope that the *Prince of Wales* may one day have the honour of another visit.

Yours sincerely
John Leach[124]

It is believed that Leach kept the photograph in his quarters in *Prince of Wales* for the rest of his life.

CHAPTER X

THE ROYAL NAVY CAPTAIN AND THE AMERICANS

Captain Leach was not what many Americans assumed a British officer to be; he was devoid of any affectation, much less pomposity. His first real contact with the US Navy was on the China Station from 1936–1938 when he was captain of HMS *Cumberland*. The American ship that he encountered most often was USS *Augusta*. Both ships were heavy cruisers and their captains had much in common, being the products of proud naval traditions.

It is unknown how often Captain Leach entertained Captain Harold V. McKittrick of USS *Augusta*, but it can be assumed that McKittrick did his best to reciprocate. Those officers who were fortunate enough to be invited for cocktails and dinner in *Cumberland* surely enjoyed themselves much more than their British counterparts when they were entertained aboard USS *Augusta*, since the US Navy prohibited any alcohol on its ships. One of the most memorable of Captain Leach's social contacts with the US Navy took place outside Manila on 14 January 1937. This is described in Patrick Boniface's *Chronicle of HMS Cumberland*:

> The Americans, who ran the US Navy Base at Cavite, seven miles outside of Manila, welcomed the British cruiser on 14 January. *Cumberland* anchored inside the breakwater and sent boats ashore full of crew members eager for some rest and relaxation. The US Forces in the Philippines

laid on a full programme of entertainment and sports. One of the best attended was the Santa Anna Cabaret which was the largest dancehall in the world. On one evening the British Club entertained some 300 sailors and about 3,000 gallons of beer was drunk.[125]

Boniface does not explain how these Jack Tars managed to consume 10 gallons per person.

When Harry Hopkins crossed the Atlantic four-and-a-half years later as a passenger in HMS *Prince of Wales*, he was not at his best. He was still recovering from an exhausting trip to Russia, suffering from the effects of colon surgery and was probably violently seasick for most of the voyage. With his arduous duties Captain Leach had virtually no time for social amenities. It is regrettable that the two men had little time to become acquainted. He spent more time with Hopkins' master President Roosevelt when the latter attended divine service on 10 August 1941 (see previous chapter). He was the first to greet the American, who had a keen interest in naval history, particularly naval engagements between the British and the Germans. He clearly wanted to have a chat with Leach about the battle with the *Bismarck*.

Captain Leach also greeted General George Catlett Marshall – who would become America's greatest General – and Admiral Ernest J. King, who was destined to head the US Navy during the coming war but whose prejudice against the British and the Royal Navy hardly enhanced Anglo-American relations. Admiral of the Fleet Viscount Cunningham later wrote of King, 'A man of immense capacity and ability, quite ruthless in his methods, he was not an easy person to get on with.'[126] Another American admiral whom Leach met that day was Admiral Harold Stark who since 1939 had been Chief of Naval Operations. In less than eight months he would take command of all US Naval Forces in the European area with his headquarters in London. He always worked well with the Royal Navy.

In the time allowed Captain Leach could only welcome each of these Americans and exchange a few pleasantries, except for one man. General Henry Arnold, known to his many friends as 'Hap' would later write:

At 4:30 (Saturday, 9 August 1941) we went aboard the *Prince of Wales* to make a boarding call and pay our respects. I had an opportunity to become acquainted with Captain John Leach, her commander, who had fought her against the *Bismarck* …[127]

Leach and Arnold had much to discuss. On 21 July 1921 General 'Billy' Mitchell's aircraft, using 1,000lb bombs, had sunk the battleship *Ostfriesland* off the North Carolina Cape. Only three years before the *Ostfriesland* had been one of the most important ships in the German High Seas Fleet having survived the Battle of Jutland. She had been completed only three years before the start of the First World War and had a displacement of 22,808 tons and a main armament of twelve 12-inch guns. Many in the US Army and the US Navy considered her unsinkable by aircraft because of the four separate skins of steel which covered her decks. Arnold was a close friend and ardent admirer of General Mitchell. At the time he was a junior officer at Langley Field in Texas and the sinking of the *Ostfriesland* did not go unnoticed. Arnold later wrote, 'Everybody throughout the Air Force (then still part of the Army) celebrated at Langley Field. They put planes in the air to meet the returning bombers; and every man, woman and child was down at the line to meet the men as they got out of their planes.'[128] The navy however took the sinking of the *Ostfriesland* in its stride and maintained that since the bombing did not take place under combat conditions it was inconclusive. 'The battleship was still the backbone of the fleet and the bulwark of the nation's sea defense'.[129]

The year before, Captain Leach had pondered the lessons to be learned from the Fleet Air Arm's highly successful strike against the Italian main fleet in Taranto Harbour on the night of 11 November, as mentioned briefly in Chapter VI. That night shortly after 2300 the first wave of twelve Swordfish armed with torpedoes took off from the aircraft carrier *Illustrious*. The Swordfish was quite old fashioned with its open cockpit and its ungainly fixed wings at two levels. The second wave consisted of only nine Swordfish but as a result of the combined strikes three Italian battleships were badly damaged. They were *Conte di Cavour*, *Italia* and *Caro Diulio*; *Cavour* would never go to sea again. It was perhaps the most decisive blow dealt the Italian Navy in the entire conflict and ushered in a new era in naval warfare that did not go unnoticed by the Japanese Navy. It is unclear whether Captain Leach and General Arnold discussed the sinking of *Ostfriesland* and the disabling of the three Italian battleships at Taranto but both understood the reality that the time of the battleship was nearing its end.

One other American would play a role in Captain Leach's life. Cecil Brown would reveal Captain Leach to America in a dramatic radio broadcast on 11 December 1941 and had already written about the Captain in his war diary, which was eventually published to much acclaim in 1942. Brown was a seasoned war correspondent who had covered the war in Yugoslavia – where he had been captured by the Germans – and in the western desert where he had been on the receiving end of German bombs. He had flown into Singapore on the huge flying boat *Canopus*, arriving there on 3 August 1941. Shortly after *Prince of Wales* reached Singapore on 2 December, Brown had boarded that great ship to have a long talk with her captain. Brown liked Leach immensely from the very start of their all too brief association; indeed, almost every American who met Captain Leach was taken with his candour and his charm.

Chapter XI

From Gibraltar to Singapore

During the first three years of the Second World War Britain was almost always forced to wage a defensive war. In those years, few of Britain's island fortresses were able to hold out once air superiority was lost. This was true in the battle for Crete and Britain's two principal island fortresses in the Far East, Hong Kong and Singapore. During the war only one island fortress held out despite the fact that the Luftwaffe and the Regia Aeronautica controlled the air for over two years, the island of Malta.

Malta's location 60 miles east of Sicily and 1,000 miles from British bases in Egypt as well as 1,000 miles from the British base of Gibraltar placed an enormous burden on the Royal Navy. In order to make Malta an operational base for submarines and destroyers, convoys carrying supplies from east or west had to run the gauntlet of Axis air and surface attacks. In addition to re-supplying the Malta naval base with oil and ships' supplies it was necessary to re-supply the RAF with aviation fuel, spare parts and new aircraft. The attrition in Spitfires and Hurricanes was always a major concern. The British Army maintained a permanent garrison on Malta of about 22,000 infantry and artillery men, who also had to be fully supplied (for an excellent account of the trials experienced by these men, see S.A.M. Hudson's *UXB Malta: Royal Engineers Bomb Disposal 1940–44*). On top of all these tasks the Royal

Navy had the burden of supplying food to Malta's civilian population of 270,000. The extent of German and Italian air raids on Malta is summarised in the *Oxford Companion to World War II*.

> Hitler's invasion of the USSR in June 1941 ... diverted Luftwaffe units to the German-Soviet War, but raids were renewed in December with even greater intensity. During January 1942 there were 262, during February 236, and in March and April twice the tonnage of bombs that London had suffered during the Blitz was dropped on Malta.[130]

In early September 1941 Captain Leach received orders from the Admiralty to take *Prince of Wales* to Gibraltar for the purpose of reinforcing the ships that would escort a convoy to Malta, one of only three convoys sent to the island that year. The one that involved *Prince of Wales* was given the code name Operation *Halberd*. The escort for the twelve transport and merchant ships consisted of three battleships, one aircraft carrier, five cruisers, eighteen destroyers, one corvette and nine submarines. The Commander-in-Chief, Vice Admiral Sir James Somerville, flew his flag in HMS *Nelson*. The Royal Navy's squadron permanently at Gibraltar was known as Force H, and for Operation *Halberd* it was reinforced by units from the Home Fleet including *Prince of Wales*. The fast cruisers and destroyers in Force H were given the responsibility of escorting the convoy all the way to Grand Harbour, Malta. This escort called Force X was under the command of Rear-Admiral H.M. Burrough, flying his flag in the light cruiser HMS *Kenya*. *Prince of Wales* had been added to Force H because of the possibility that the Italian Navy might attempt to redeem its defeat in the Battle of Cape Matapan with its newest battleships.

It was exceedingly fortunate that Operation *Halberd* took place in September as Admiral Doenitz had not yet ordered substantial numbers of his U-boats into the Mediterranean and Air Marshal Goering had transferred most of his Ju-87 and Ju-88 bombers from airfields in Sicily to bases near the Russian front. Thus, German strength in the Western Mediterranean was negligible. In the event, enemy opposition to Force H and Force X came entirely from the Regia Aeronautica. One of its torpedo bombers, the SIAI Marchetti SM 79 was considered outstanding. Despite the presence of Fulmar fighter aircraft from the carrier *Ark Royal* the Italians started their torpedo bomber attacks on the morning of 27 September. That day *Prince of Wales'* anti-aircraft guns were in constant use. *Prince of Wales* shot down two Italian aircraft without coming to any harm, but the flagship HMS *Nelson* was torpedoed and severely damaged. After dark on 28 September one of the merchant ships, *Imperial Star*, was torpedoed in moonlight and had to be abandoned. These losses were considered well within the acceptable limit for a Malta convoy.

Operation *Halberd* might have triggered a major engagement with the Italian Fleet. In 1938 Admiral Andrew Browne Cunningham, Commander-in-Chief of the Mediterranean Fleet, had paid a courtesy call on the flagship of Admiral Riccardi, later the Commander-in-Chief of the Italian Navy. After an elaborate luncheon, Riccardi showed his British guests his palatial cabin. He took some pride in pointing out a book on his bedside table, *The Life of Nelson*. During the war Cunningham decided that Riccardi had not profited much from his nightly reading, as after learning that Force H had departed Gibraltar obviously headed for Malta, Riccardi ordered Fleet Admiral Iachino to steam out of Naples to intercept it. Admiral Iachino's fleet consisted of only two battleships, six cruisers and fourteen destroyers as part of the Italian fleet remained in port due to fuel shortages. There are two quite different versions of what the Italian Fleet did next, the first of which comes from Admiral Cunningham, written in 1949.

Very careful preparations had been made for the defence of the convoy. Every available long-range fighter in Egypt or elsewhere on the station was sent to Malta, while all the submarines from Malta took up their stations off Naples, Taranto and north of Sicily in case the Italian Fleet came out to interfere. Actually it did emerge from Naples and came south, but made off again when Force 'H' went after it.[131]

In 1981 over 30 years later another version of events appeared in *The World Almanac of World War II* edited by Brigadier Peter Young, who had been one of Britain's most decorated soldiers. The chronology of this almanac was largely prepared by Donald Sommerville, historian of University College, Oxford. His chronology for 24–30 September 1941 reads as follows:

Mediterranean Operation *Halberd* is launched in a major effort to carry supplies from Gibraltar to Malta, there are nine transports in the convoy and their escorts and covering force include three battleships, one carrier, five cruisers and 18 destroyers. On 26 September Admiral Iachino leads two battleships, six cruisers and 14 destroyers of the Italian Fleet out to intercept. The remainder of the Italian Fleet stays in port, ostensibly because of fuel shortage. On 27 September both sides fail to find the main enemy force by air reconnaissance … the heavy ships do not make contact.[132]

Given that Sommerville wrote this 40 years after the incident and had access to more information than did Admiral Cunningham, it would seem likely that his version of events is more accurate. There remains an unanswered question. Why would Admiral Riccardi risk the almost certain destruction of two battleships by a superior British force? It is conceivable that he hoped to lure Force H close to the Italian mainland where it could be assailed by waves of torpedo bombers. If the Italians had succeeded in sinking any British capital ships with their torpedo bombers, it might well have dispelled the conviction in certain circles of the Royal Navy that battleships manoeuvring in the open sea could defend themselves from torpedo bombers without fighter aircraft.

Geoffrey Brooke, who was aboard *Prince of Wales* for her entire life, would become one of her best chroniclers. Of her involvement in Operation *Halberd*, he wrote:

> The ship's first encounter with hostile aircraft had certainly gone well. The whole operation had, in fact, exceeded all hopes and the double success provided yet another fillip to the confidence and already high spirits of *Prince of Wales*. She sailed later that evening to arrive at Scapa on October 6.[133]

On 16 October, from an unknown location in home waters, Leach wrote to Churchill.

My Dear Prime Minister,

On behalf of myself and the other three officers of the Prince of Wales who recently received awards for their service I write to thank you most sincerely for your kind message of congratulations which was most thoroughly appreciated.

I have not yet seen the full list and consequently do not know if any of my ship's company appear in it. But I will pass on your kind message to them in due course, should any of their names be included.

The *Prince of Wales* flourishes and I believe that big strides have been made in the reliability of the main armament machinery since you were on board. I hope in the near future to have an opportunity of confirming this view.

I do so much wish that you had been on board during Operation 'Halberd'. There were sights to be seen which would have rejoiced your heart and the whole operation was an invaluable experience for us. The *Prince of Wales* hopes that you are well and sends her best wishes for your continued prosperity.

Yours Sincerely,
John Leach[134]

In the autumn of 1941 the Prime Minister and the First Sea Lord debated long and hard over whether two capital ships accompanied by an air-craft carrier should be sent to Singapore as a deterrent to the Japanese. Churchill won the debate, but in the judgment of most historians he made a strategic error of the first magnitude.

There is an American aspect of this debate that is largely unknown. Based on their cables to one another that autumn it seems beyond question that at Placentia Bay Roosevelt and Churchill had reached some understanding about sending reinforcements to the Far East in an effort to deter a Japanese attack. The earliest possible deployment would have had to involve British battleships and American heavy bombers. Historians have made little mention of their understanding because of the absence of archival evidence.

Admiral Sir Tom Phillips was named Commander-in-Chief of the squadron that was meant to deter the Japanese. This squadron would consist of HMS *Prince of Wales* and HMS *Repulse* together with an escort of four destroyers. The new fleet carrier, HMS *Indomitable*, had been designated to be part of this squadron, but she had run aground off Jamaica in early November and was unable to join *Prince of Wales* and *Repulse* in time. No other British carriers were available.

While Phillips never lacked courage and was obviously intelligent, his judgment was flawed. In 1938 the British plan for the defence of Hong

Kong was referred to as 'Standard C'. It involved a British presence that retained no more than a mere foothold on Hong Kong Island, but which would deny the Japanese any anchorage. After Phillips became Deputy Chief of the Naval Staff he sent a minute to the First Sea Lord, Sir Dudley Pound, which was both dramatic and foolhardy:

> I have always felt that this decision to adopt Standard 'C' was fundamentally wrong and not in accordance with our position as a great maritime Power. Hong Kong is our most exposed outpost and ought to be properly defended with 15-inch guns and everything else we can put there. No other country would leave an outpost of this nature in an undefended state.[135]

Admiral Phillips had no recent sea experience and had never been in a ship that had to defend herself from attack by enemy aircraft. Both in appearance and in personality Admiral Phillips and Captain Leach were almost complete opposites. The Admiral was diminutive, standing only five feet two inches to Leach's six feet two inches, and he lacked the latter's charm. They did share, however, a total commitment to their mission. They both knew that if deterrence failed, they would have to engage both the Japanese Navy and the Japanese Air Force under circumstances that highly favoured the enemy.

Admiral Phillips had already acquired a reputation for having the sharpest mind in the Royal Navy. On 18 May 1940 John Colville, then Churchill's youngest private secretary, wrote in his diary, 'the position [in France] is still critical, and Admiral Phillips, the best brain in the Navy, asserts to the P.M. that the Cabinet have now got to take a fundamental decision.'[136] Unfortunately, this exalted reputation did not make Admiral Phillips a better admiral.

The name Hastings Ismay suggests a mysterious character in a British spy novel. In the Second World War he was in fact a highly regarded general in the British Army. Those who knew him best called him 'Pug' after the small Chinese dog breed with a snub nose and wrinkled face. To quote John Colville, Ismay 'was the main channel of communication between Churchill and the Chiefs of Staff, of whose committee he was a full member, and he was equally trusted by both.'[137] Ismay was devastated when the news reached Whitehall that both *Prince of Wales* and *Repulse* had been lost and he grieved for Tom Phillips. Nevertheless, when the time came for him to write his wartime memoirs, Ismay did not unnecessarily eulogise his friend.

Tom Phillips had been successively Director of Plans, Deputy Chief of Naval Staff, and Vice-Chief of Naval Staff of the Admiralty. We had worked together for many years in peace and war, and I had always greatly admired his courage, industry, integrity and professional competence. His whole heart and soul were in the Navy, and he believed that there was nothing that he could not do. In particular, he refused to admit that properly armed and well-fought ships had anything to fear from air power. Nor was he alone in that opinion. Even Winston Churchill, whose forecasts were not often at fault, was one of the many who did not 'believe that well-built modern warships properly defended by armour and A–A guns were likely to fall a prey to hostile aircraft.' The battles-royal which raged between Tom Phillips and Arthur Harris [later Marshal of the Royal Air Force Sir Arthur Harris] when they were Directors of Plans in their respective departments were never-ending, and always inconclusive. On one occasion, when the situation which would arise in the event of Italy entering the war on the side of Germany was under discussion, Tom Phillips insisted that our Fleet would have free use of the Mediterranean, however strong the Italian Air Force might be. Bert Harris exploded, 'One day, Tom, you will be standing on a box on your bridge (Tom was diminutive in stature) and your ship will be smashed to pieces by bombers and torpedo aircraft. As she sinks, your last words will be, 'That was a … great mine!'[138]

On 24 October 1941 *Prince of Wales* steamed out of the Firth of Clyde after taking Admiral Phillips and his staff aboard at Greenock. Her second port of call was Cape Town, South Africa. Pound had told Churchill he would make a final decision on whether to send *Prince of Wales* on to Singapore after she reached Cape Town; however, it seems clear enough in hindsight that Pound had already lost the debate.

On 10 November 1941 Churchill gave a speech at the Lord Mayor's Day Luncheon at the Mansion House, London. It was an unmistakable war warning to Japan. After first talking about conditions in occupied Europe and the improvements over the last year in Britain's military situation, Churchill turned to the Far East. After making reference to the sinking of the *Bismarck* and the cowing of the Italian Navy, he revealed that Britain was strong enough to provide a naval force of heavy ships in the Indian and Pacific Oceans. He asserted that the movement of these naval forces was in conjunction with the US Main Fleet.

Despite Japan's four-year war with China that had been characterised by the most despicable acts of barbarism, Churchill spoke with politeness and considerable restraint. He pointed out that he had voted for the 1902 treaty between Britain and Japan. He spoke of himself as being a sentimental well wisher to the Japanese and an admirer of their many gifts and qualities, but in his next breath he revealed his total commitment to the special relationship with the US. He told his listeners and his wider audience in the US and Japan, that in the event that the two countries went to war, the British declaration of war would follow within the hour. In the entire history of Anglo-American relations no previous Prime Minister had ever committed Britain to a war to defend American life and liberty.

Churchill tried hard to convince the Japanese of the utter folly of a war with the US by contrasting the industrial strength of the two countries. He pointed out that America produced around 90,000,000 tons of steel annually whereas Japan only produced around 7,000,000 tons. He also vowed to protect British interests in the Far East and expressed his admiration for the Chinese people in defending their homeland.

Churchill's speech omitted any reference to the very real Japanese threat to the Netherlands East Indies. He had been unable to get Roosevelt to make an unequivocal statement that it was in American's vital interest to protect the Dutch colony. For the Japanese the vital issue was oil, not steel. Japanese domestic production only provided a fraction of the oil needed by the Imperial Japanese Navy. The nearest source of oil was the Netherlands East Indies. In 1940 that colony produced nearly 60 million barrels of oil per annum, more than any other country in Asia.

After the Netherlands was overrun by the German Army in five days, Japan saw an opportunity to gain the upper hand over a weak colony. With no hope of survival without British or American intervention, the Dutch colony extended every courtesy to Japan's so called chief trade negotiator, Kenkichi Yoshizawa. At the conclusion of his mission he was given an opulent farewell banquet by Governor General von Starkenborgh-Stachouwer and his American-born wife. Their long dinner table was beautifully appointed with fine crystal and china. The Governor General's wife was the only lady at the table. The 30 men were formally attired in dinner jackets or military dress uniforms and sixteen barefooted servants hovered in the background. To all appearances this was a glittering social occasion to honour Yoshizawa; in reality it was little more than a face saving gesture. While the colony finally agreed to increase its oil exports to Japan, they refused to yield to Japanese demands that their entire economy be placed under Japanese control.

Churchill's 'war warning' to Japan on 11 November 1941 utterly failed to deter Japanese aggression. The military oligarchy that ruled Japan were convinced that the Japanese was destined to be the masters of all of Asia and that oil was essential to success in their war with China and in their inevitable future wars with Britain and the US.

On the 23-day cruise to Cape Town, *Prince of Wales* had no contacts with U-boats or enemy aircraft and Leach was able to catch up with some personal correspondence. One of his surviving letters is a hand-written note to General Sir John Dill, Chief of the Imperial General Staff, which is dated 15 November, the day before his ship reached Cape Town. The two had become acquainted on the voyage to Placentia Bay three months before.

Thank you so much for your note. I do think it was good of you, with all of your innumerable activities, to find time to write to me … We are certainly getting our fair share of excitement and change … I hope you are fit and flourishing. Thank you again so much for your letter.

Yours Sincerely,
John Leach[139]

It was extraordinary for the Chief of the Imperial General Staff to take the time to write to Leach. Clearly the two men had the beginnings of a friendship.

Before her departure from Cape Town, *Prince of Wales* received a welcome addition to her anti-aircraft armament in the form of a single 40mm Bofors. 26 November 1941 was the penultimate day of *Prince of Wales*' ten-day voyage from Cape Town to Colombo. Because of the publicity surrounding *Prince of Wales*' arrival in Cape Town, not to mention her highly visible presence in the harbour, the Japanese were well aware of her movements. There is little reason to believe that the Japanese did not take note of her stopover in Colombo.

Halfway across the Pacific in Hawaii, on the other side of the International Date Line, personnel from the Japanese Consulate in Honolulu kept close track of US Navy ships entering or leaving Pearl Harbor. On most days the Japanese at the Consulate knew precisely which battleships and carriers were at their moorings. This information was coded and transmitted to Tokyo.

26 November 1941 was the day that 30 Japanese warships, including six aircraft carriers, departed from remote Hitokappu Bay in the Kurile Islands which lie north of the Japanese Home Islands. With the possible exception of personnel in the Far East Combined Bureau, which will be discussed in the next chapter, neither the Royal Navy nor the US Navy had the slightest knowledge of this furtive movement, which represented the most powerful naval strike force in the Pacific or any other ocean. In retrospect this was the first day of the final countdown to disaster for the US Navy at Pearl Harbor and for the Royal Navy in the South China Sea.

On arrival at Colombo Admiral Phillips and his key staff disembarked and were immediately flown to Singapore to confer with the service chiefs there. Leach then took his ship south of Ceylon to rendezvous with *Repulse* under the command of Captain W.G. Tennant, a close friend, who was his senior in rank. The remainder of Leach's journey to Singapore was much more relaxed. He now had total authority over his own ship, was under the command of a trusted friend and the two ships were no longer in an active war zone. He could also look forward to a very special reunion; his son Henry was a midshipman in the light cruiser HMS *Mauritius*, refitting at Singapore. Perhaps the only enervating aspect of their journey across the Indian Ocean was the weather. *Prince of Wales'* company were experiencing tropical heat that they had not known before.

As mentioned in the previous chapter, an American war correspondent called Cecil Brown had arrived in Singapore on Sunday 3 August. Brown, who had been expelled from Italy by Mussolini's government and arrested by the German Army in Yugoslavia, was totally committed to Britain's cause. He was destined to write the most famous firsthand account of *Prince of Wales'* and *Repulse's* final action. On his arrival in Singapore he checked in at Raffles Hotel.

I had dinner tonight in the beautiful palm-lined courtyard of Raffles Hotel. Each table, set on the grass, had a pink shaded lamp and a vase of orchids. The Argyle and Sutherland Highlanders band played for the smartly dressed officials and women in gay print dresses. The members of the band wore plaid hats and white coats and kilts, and the war seemed a million miles away.[140]

The legendary Raffles Hotel, named after Sir Stamford Raffles, the Englishman who founded the City of the Lion on a site that had been a mangrove swamp, was for many synonymous with Singapore. The long bar, known as Cad's Alley, attracted all types including rubber planters, sea captains and sundry adventurers. It was renowned for the 'Singapore gin sling' – two ounces of gin, one of cherry brandy, a dash of Cointreau, lemon juice and bitters.

Raffles's legend grew in part from its literary guests. Joseph Conrad is said to have been sitting on one of its verandas when he read a report in the *Straits Times* of a foundering ship whose crew had left hundreds of native passengers to their fate. Supposedly this story inspired him to write *Lord Jim*. Somerset Maugham, who spent a good bit of his life in south-east Asia, has been quoted as saying, 'Raffles stood for all the fables of the exotic East.' Noel Coward, called Singapore 'a first class place for second class people.'

Singapore is situated only a few degrees north of the equator. The heat and the humidity created an unhealthy environment for most Caucasians until they were acclimatised. Before his father's arrival Midshipman Leach had seen the effect on the Army garrison with whom he billeted while his ship was in dry dock. 'Subalterns of the Regiment with which I stayed spent their working hours (0900 to 1300) riding motor bicycles around the rugger field ("always useful to be able to carry a dispatch").'[141] The younger Leach also wrote of the wealth and poverty that he saw in Singapore. 'The island is full of contrasts in the modern high-rise blocks of the business and shopping centres, and the rustic simplicity of the picturesque native kampongs; the impeccable bungalows of the well-to-do, and the squalid ramshackle huts of shanty town ...'[142]

Both Cecil Brown and Midshipman Henry Leach had the opportunity to assess the situation in Singapore in the final months preceding the Japanese onslaught. Independently each came to the same troubling conclusion: the whole military establishment seemed to be lethargic and complacent to a degree that could not be explained by the climate or the remoteness of Britain's war with Germany and Italy. In retrospect much of the blame can be attributed to lack of rigorous, dynamic leadership by the Commander-in-Chief, Air Chief Marshal Sir Robert Brooke-Popham. Like other British and American senior commanders Brooke-Popham underestimated the Japanese threat. On 3 December he held an off-the-record conference for about 30 correspondents who included Cecil Brown. Brooke-Popham's remarks revealed a rather limited understanding of both Japanese capabilities and intentions. Brown, who took copious notes, wrote the following:

> I asked Sir Robert, 'What is Japan going to do?' 'Although Japan does not have any particular affection for Germany, being on the initiative, she is quite likely to copy Germany's methods whenever applicable,' Sir Robert said. 'That is, to strike at the weakness, rather than strength, and accomplish her objectives by intimidations rather than war.'

...

> 'What do you think is going to happen?' I asked again. 'Well, Sir Robert said, 'We are looking about, wondering what Japan is going to do. Japan doesn't seem to have a policy of what to do step by step. You know there are signs of defence steps too. She is doing things in Indo-China to defend herself there. Japan is beginning to be afraid she is going to be attacked.'

...

> Kennard of the Malaya Broadcasting asked how American planes compared with Japanese. 'Oh, we are not worried about that,' Sir Robert said. 'But what about these Brewster Buffaloes – are they good enough?' 'They could give a very good account of themselves,' Sir Robert assured us. 'Don't you think that we need some of the machines that Britain has at home?' 'Oh no,' Sir Robert said scornfully. 'If we need any of these super Spitfires and hyper Hurricanes we can get them out here quick enough.'[143]

The arrival of *Prince of Wales* and other unidentified heavy units of the Royal Navy at Singapore was publicised, primarily for the benefit of Japan. On 2 December *Prince of Wales* and *Repulse* reached the Singapore Naval Base shortly after 17.30 to find a large crowd eagerly awaiting them. There is a photograph of Admiral Phillips, his chief of staff Rear Admiral Palliser and his young staff officer for plans, Commander Michael Goodenough, watching their arrival. Phillips wears a particularly stern expression. Duff and Diana Cooper were part of the crowd. In August Churchill had decided to send Cooper, the erstwhile First Lord of the Admiralty, to Singapore to report directly to him on the situation. By 1 November Cooper had completed his report and he sent his aide Tony Keswick to London with instructions to deliver it personally to the Prime Minister. This report would soon become irrelevant. Cooper, who was always devoted to the Royal Navy, observed the arrival of *Prince of Wales* and *Repulse* with pride.

> It was a great moment when they came around the bend into the narrow waters of the straits that divide Singapore from the mainland. We were all at the naval base to welcome them, and they arrived punctual to the minute with their escort of four destroyers. They conferred a sense of complete security.[144]

It is inexplicable that these two ships would have 'conferred a sense of complete security' on a former First Lord of the Admiralty.

On 4 December Admiral Phillips, accompanied by three of his naval staff officers, left Singapore by seaplane for a conference in Manila with the senior US commanders, General Douglas MacArthur and Admiral Thomas C. Hart. That night Admiral Phillips' aircraft landed at Labuan Island six miles off the west coast of North Borneo where the Admiral dined and spent the night at Government House. His host was Hugh Humphrey, the British resident whose other roles included the post of naval reporting officer. It was a serene setting on a tropical evening far removed from the cares of the world. 'At dinner Humphrey asked Phillips whether there would be a war with Japan and received the answer, "I don't think so."'[145] Phillips apparently did not elaborate, but one can surmise that he, like Churchill, could not bring himself to believe that the rulers of Japan would do something so foolhardy.

Henry and his father had not seen one another for more than a year and had had no time to discuss the battle with the *Bismarck*, the voyage with Churchill or the action in the Mediterranean. Beyond that there was much that Henry wanted to share with his father about his life in the Royal Navy. Henry's first opportunity to visit his father was on Saturday evening, 6 December on board *Prince of Wales*. (Because of the International Date Line, Singapore was one day ahead of London, Washington and Pearl Harbor.) Being accustomed to the strict dress code of the Royal Navy, Henry dressed in the evening uniform equivalent to a dinner jacket. To his surprise Henry discovered that his father, who was always meticulous about the dress code, was still wearing his white tropical uniform consisting of an open neck shirt and shorts.

Admiral Phillips had not yet returned from his meeting in Manila with General MacArthur and Admiral Hart; this meant that the Admiral's dining quarters were available. While Leach had the option of taking his son to dinner in the wardroom with the other officers, he preferred to dine in private. Before dinner they had a chance to talk in the captain's cabin where Leach had been writing a letter to his wife, Evelyn, at his roll-top desk. He handed the last page of the letter to Henry who added a note to his mother.

Henry was offered a cigarette with the comment, 'I don't know what bad habits you've fallen into this year.'[146] After they had talked about family matters, their conversation turned to naval subjects. Leach asked his son about *Mauritius*'s RDF (Radio Direction Finding). This was a reference to what would be renamed radar. Henry had served in *Mauritius* for nine months and had kept watch regularly on the bridge, but he had never even heard of RDF.

The approaching war in the Pacific was foremost in Leach's mind. Referring to the mounting Japanese threat, he asked his son, 'What d'you make of the situation out here?'[147] Like other midshipmen Henry had total confidence in the Royal Navy. He replied, 'Let 'em come … Let's have a crack at them.'[148] With a grave look his father quietly said, 'I don't think you have any idea of the enormity of the odds we are up against.'[149]

That night, the final Saturday night of peace, the smartly dressed ladies and gentlemen at Raffles carried on as if nothing would ever change.

CHAPTER XII

SIGNALS INTELLIGENCE THAT FAILED
AND HUMAN INTELLIGENCE THAT COULD HAVE SUCCEEDED

Hong Kong Island was ceded to Britain in 1840 after the Opium War and twenty years later the Convention of Peking added the Kowloon Peninsula and Stonecutter's Island. Stonecutter's Island was less than a mile off the west coast of Kowloon and approximately three miles due north of Victoria, the capital of Hong Kong, one of the small, seemingly unimportant dependencies around the Island.

Like countless other captains in the Royal Navy, Captain Leach sailed many times through the passage between Stonecutter's Island and Hong Kong, which encompassed approximately 32 square miles. Since there was a small Royal Navy facility on Stonecutter's, he may have visited the island. In 1935 Stonecutter's became extraordinarily important because that year the British created a top-secret wireless station on the island which could intercept a huge volume of Japanese naval signals. These included signals between Commander-in-Chief of Japan's Combined Fleet Admiral Isoroku Yamamoto and the Combined Fleet, as well as a wide variety of other naval signals from ships or shore installations. This intelligence gathering was carried out by an organisation called the Far East Combined Bureau (FECB), a joint command of the Royal Navy, the Army and the Royal Air Force. Their headquarters was in Hong Kong where they continued to operate until 1939 when it was deemed too vulnerable to a Japanese attack. Over the summer and autumn of

1939 it relocated to Singapore except for the staff manning the intercept station at Stonecutter's Island who remained there until just before the Japanese captured the island on 11 December 1941. Almost two years earlier the FECB had established another powerful intercept station in Singapore.

Prior to 1991 references to the FECB in the Second World War histories were few and far between; Churchill's six-volume history of the conflict contains not a single reference. *The Japanese Thrust* by Lionel Wigmore makes only three minor references in footnotes, which quote Compton Mackenzie's *Eastern Epic* 'General Percival ... was depending for his judgment about Japanese intentions and Japanese fighting efficiency on the Far East Combined Bureau ...'[150] In 1979, the official British intelligence historian F.H. Hinsley wrote *British Intelligence in the Second World War,* which contains an oblique reference to FECB stating that as of September 1939, 'It remained possible ... to keep track of [IJN's] main naval movements.'[151] This footnote must be read in light of his disclaimer in the Preface where he states, '... there are unavoidable omissions. The most important of these is that we have not attempted to cover the war in the Far East.'[152]

The 1995 *The Oxford Companion to World War II* devoted two paragraphs to the Far East Combined Bureau[153] written by the general editor, I.C.B. Dear, a former officer in the Royal Marines. Dear writes, 'The FECB's records were probably destroyed and opinions vary as to how much the Bureau contributed to breaking the Japanese Navy's JN-25 cipher ...'[153] One can only assume that if the records of this intelligence bureau had not been located by 1995, then they will never be discovered. Dear would have been aware of a controversial book first published in 1991 entitled *Betrayal at Pearl Harbor – How Churchill Lured Roosevelt into World War II.* The co-authors James Rusbridger and Eric Nave assert that Churchill knew that a Japanese task force was headed for Pearl Harbor and that he failed to warn Roosevelt. Rusbridger and Nave claim that on 25 November 1941 the FECB intercepted a signal from Admiral Yamamoto, Commander-in-Chief of the Combined Fleet, to Admiral Naguma, Commander-in-Chief of the First Carrier Strike Force, which read, 'the Task Force will move out of Hitokappu Wan [Tankan Bay] on the morning of 26 November and advance to the standing-by position on the afternoon of 4 December and speedily complete refuelling.'[154] In the Preface written by Rusbridger he asserts that by 26 November Commander Malcolm Burnett RN 'had personally advised Churchill in London that the only logical target for the impending attack was Pearl Harbor.'[155]

The co-authors were a curious pair. Rusbridger had written two earlier books both of which were controversial, *The Intelligence Game* and *Who Sank Surcouf?* Eric Nave had distinguished service in the Royal Navy and the Royal Australian Navy. In 1988 Nave, who was 90 at the time, was living in Melbourne when he received a telephone call from Rusbridger who told Nave that he had come across his name in the unpublished diary of one Howard Baker who had been in Java before the war; the diary had 'an intriguing reference to an Australian naval officer called Commander Nave, who had broken the Japanese naval codes before the war.'[156] Rusbridger flew out to Australia and spent days recording interviews with Nave. It is highly unlikely that Nave was much involved in either the research or writing of *Betrayal at Pearl Harbor*, which was extensive, and the publisher's editor had to turn 'a long technical manuscript into final concise print'.[157]

Besides claiming that Churchill knew in advance from the aforesaid FECB intercept of 25 November 1941, and from later intercepts, that a giant Japanese strike force of aircraft carriers was at sea headed for Pearl Harbor, the book also claims that following the Japanese surrender Churchill sent secret instructions to FECB headquarters in Ceylon to destroy all of its archives. On both claims their book is a failure. The first depends on the alleged FECB intercepts and the uncorroborated statements of Commander Malcolm Burnett, OBE, RN to an historian named Dr Andrew Gordon. Burnett died on 17 July 1984 three years before Rusbridger decided to write his book and it seems unlikely that either co-author interviewed Dr Gordon, who is never quoted. There is a brief reference to Commander Burnett's widow that requires comment. Rusbridger asserts in the Preface that after the first edition to their book was published, certain memories were awakened, including that of Commander Burnett's widow, Mary. It is claimed that in December 1991 she appeared on American television and confirmed what her late husband had told Dr Gordon. Neither the television station nor the television programme is identified. Rusbridger makes no claim that he interviewed Mary Burnett and every statement that Rusbridger has attributed to Commander Burnett is unverifiable.

The claim that Churchill instructed FECB to destroy its archives after Japan's surrender is even more untenable. The co-authors cite as their source Lieutenant Commander W. W. Mortimer, RNR (Ret.). Mortimer is never quoted directly and what he actually said to the co-authors will never be known. One of the co-authors (probably Rusbridger) added this aside, 'Whether Churchill had the authority to do this seems doubtful...'[158] Churchill did not have the authority since he was no longer prime minister at the time of Japan's surrender and it is regrettable that Rusbridger chose to make these claims against Churchill the main focus of his book.

Correlli Barnett's book *Engage the Enemy More Closely: the Royal Navy in the Second World War* contains some scathing criticism of Churchill as First Lord of the Admiralty and as Prime Minister but no mention of Churchill knowing about the attack on Pearl Harbor. Barnett describes Britain's woeful lack of intelligence about Japanese operational plans for war against Britain and the US throughout 1941 as follows:

> The British in particular, last in line to receive gleanings from 'Magic' and then by no means all of them, could only guess, grope and argue about Japanese intentions and plans – the Joint Intelligence Committee, the Foreign Office and Sir Robert Craigie, the ambassador in Tokyo, the Foreign Secretary and Prime Minister themselves.[159]

In stark contrast Rusbridger and Nave claim the Far East Combined Bureau was able to intercept and read virtually every important signal of the Imperial Japanese Navy at least until 4 December 1941. Without giving precise dates they describe FECB's achievements in the first years of its operations as follows:

> FECB read all the Japanese messages with ease and had prior knowledge of every operation they planned. The first advice usually came after a War Cabinet meeting in Tokyo and would be sent in the Commander-in-Chief's code. A typical message would read, 'Instructions have been issued for the capture of Canton. This will be known as Operation Y. Further details will be given by Chief of Naval Staff.' This immediately helped FECB identify the much longer messages that would shortly be intercepted in the Blue Book code. These would give precise details of the number of transports, escorting warships, the Army units involved, landing place, route to be taken, and so forth. Not a single message escaped the

listening post in Hong Kong. The powerful intercept station at Stonecutter's sucked up everything transmitted from Japan and by any ship at sea.[160]

On 1 June 1939 the Japanese Navy introduced a new code system; however, FECB and GCCS (Government Code & Cipher School), which by the autumn of 1939 had moved to its wartime home at Bletchley Park some 50 miles northwest of London, soon broke this new code. According to Rusbridger and Nave:

So by the end of 1939, GCCS and FECB could read JN-25, used between navy headquarters in Tokyo and all their ships and shore stations; the naval attaché traffic, which was still using the Red Machine; the Commander-in-Chief's code; and several other low-grade codes, such as the Appointments Code, which contained little of importance.[161]

With respect to the critical period just before Pearl Harbor and the simultaneous Japanese attacks on Northern Malaya, Singapore and Hong Kong, Rusbridger and Nave write:

The exact total of messages sent by Yamamoto between 20 November and 7 December to his Task Force at Tankan Bay, and later while at sea en route to Pearl Harbor is not known, because all Japanese naval records were destroyed before the end of the war. But at least twenty such messages were intercepted and exist today in the National Archives, Washington D.C. thus proving beyond any doubt that radio silence with the Task Force was broken after it had assembled and sailed ... The American intercepts all bear postwar decryption dates ... but Nave is adamant that every message intercepted by the Americans would also have been intercepted by the British, and because JN-25 had been broken by him since the autumn of 1939, *all* these intercepted messages would have been read without difficulty or delay by FECB and GCCS.[162]

They identify two Japanese signals of the highest importance allegedly intercepted and read by FECB on 20 November and on 25 November.

One of the first, decoded by FECB on 20 November, was from Yamamoto in Tokyo, using his combined Fleet C in C call sign, KE RO 88, to his Task

Force waiting at Tankan Bay. Here for the first time in print is the signal that effectively set in motion the war in the Pacific: 'This dispatch is top secret. To be decoded only by an officer. This order effective as of the date within the text to follow: At 0000 (midnight) on 21 November, repeat 21 November, carry out second phase for opening hostilities.'

The prefixes at the start of this message, which was known to FECB because they could read JN-25, showed that it was addressed to the Second Fleet (YA KI 4), the Third Fleet (E MU 6), the Fourth Fleet (O RE 1), the Combined Fleet (RI TA 3) and the Eleventh Air Fleet (SU YO 4), indicating that a large group of warships, including carriers, had assembled somewhere as part of the first phase of opening hostilities, and that the second phase was about to begin.[163]

Regarding the signal of 25 November, previously quoted, Rusbridger and Nave write:

> On 25 November FECB decrypted Yamamoto's next set of instruc-
> tions to his waiting Task Force in JN-25: 'The Task Force will move out
> of Hitokappu Wan [Tankan Bay] on the morning of 26 November and
> advance to the standing-by position on the afternoon of 4 December and
> speedily complete refuelling.[164]

While Rusbridger and Nave give FECB full credit for intercepting and reading both of the aforesaid signals, the source notes reveal that they had relied on quite a different source – the National Archives in Washington DC. Moreover, the National Archives records reveal that the 20 November intercept was not decrypted until 26 November 1945. The source of the 25 November intercept was also the National Archives, but it was not an intercept at all, but instead a document recovered from the wreck of the Japanese cruiser *Nachi* that was sunk in Manila Bay in November 1944. These inconsistencies alone cast doubt on their claims that Churchill had been forewarned by FECB of the attack on Pearl Harbor.

Rusbridger's book is replete with numerous source notes. It also contains in the Appendices verbatim copies of documents, some of which are marked 'top secret'. Nevertheless, the sources that he has cited and the verbatim documents that he has reproduced fail to include any original sources relating to Far East Combined Bureau except for a very few retired officers concerning events that had taken place more than 40 years earlier. Rusbridger obviously considered his co-author, Eric Nave, his most important individual source.

Eric Nave joined the Australian Navy in 1917 at the age of eighteen. Two years later he was eligible to sit for his examination for promotion to sub lieutenant and chose to study Japanese for his required foreign language. The GCCS (British Government Code & Cipher School) became aware of his fluency in Japanese and his promise at code and cipher breaking. In mid 1927 at its request Nave was loaned to the Royal Navy to work for this code breaking school and by the end of 1930 he was its most experienced Japanese code breaker and was invited to transfer from the RAN to the Royal Navy. The *London Gazette* on the front page of its issue for 2 December1930 announced that by special order of King George V, Nave had been transferred from the RAN to the Royal Navy effective 27 November 1930. In 1937 the Government Code & Cipher School sent Nave to Hong Kong to continue his work at Far East Combined Bureau. He arrived there in the autumn of 1937 only a few months after Japan had started its offensives against China's coastal cities.

Nave soon became a key figure at the interception station on Stonecutter's Island and at the headquarters of FECB in the naval dockyards on Hong Kong Island. Because the Japanese naval Code (JN-25) was periodically altered, GCCS and FECB coordinated their best efforts to break the altered code. In the autumn of 1939 Commander Malcolm Burnett RN flew out from London 'to FECB to give Nave the reconstructed dictionary and current keys'[165] to the reconstructed JN-25 codebook.

Since Hong Kong was much more vulnerable to a Japanese attack than Singapore, the headquarters of FECB was relocated to Singapore in August 1939 but the Stonecutter's Island facility continued to intercept Japanese naval signals.

It was not until 2006 that a retired officer in the Royal Australian Navy, Ian Pfennigwerth, wrote Nave's biography. *A Man of Intelligence: The Life of Captain Eric Nave, Australian Codebreaker Extraordinary* was first published in Australia in 2006. Pfennigwerth served in the Royal Australian Navy for 35 years, the last ten of which were spent primarily in the intelligence sphere; he served as Director of Naval Intelligence for three years. His book on Nave was clearly motivated by a desire to set the record straight and to celebrate 'the magnificent work done by this Australian'.[166] Pfennigwerth writes convincingly about Nave's brilliance both in his ability to break Japanese Naval codes and in his translating ability. He is also convincing about the success of the intercept station on Stonecutter's Island from October 1937 until February 1940 when Nave served with the FECB.

In a 1989 BBC interview Nave spoke of the signals intelligence that originated from Stonecutter's Island.

> The reception there in China, and particularly from Hong Kong, Stonecutter's, was excellent. We could read Tokyo [Radio] twenty-four hours a day; and the possibility of missing an important dispatch, I think, just didn't exist. Atmospherics, of course, was one thing; but we generally could overcome that. We could get static very bad at times. It was difficult, yes; but for the most part we were not in a position where you could miss a certain period during the day, or a whole message at any time. You had confidence that you could read all the traffic.[167]

In February 1940 Nave was sent to Australia on sick leave suffering from a rare illness called Tropical Sprue. At that time the cause was unknown and there was no satisfactory treatment; however, living outside the tropics clearly improved a patient's chances of recovery. Eric and his wife Helena embarked at Singapore on a Dutch ship for the voyage to Australia in February 1940. The significance of that date is that it represented the end of his work with Far East Combined Bureau, but Rusbridger's and Nave's book suggests that Nave was privy to the work of FECB in the months and weeks leading up to the Japanese attacks on 7 December. In fact Nave was over four thousand miles from Singapore for at least twenty months before the start of the Pacific war. It is unlikely that Nave had any first-hand knowledge of the FECB's code breaking operations at any time after February 1940.

In Australia Nave was able to render invaluable service to the newly created Special Intelligence Bureau, which he commanded before Pearl Harbor; yet Pfennigwerth found no involvement by Nave or Special Intelligence Bureau in any intercepts that would show that the IJN had a powerful strike force of aircraft carriers headed toward Pearl Harbor.

> It can be confidently stated that Eric Nave and the Special Intelligence Bureau had nothing at all to do with the alleged intelligence 'failures' that might have given warning of Japanese intentions to attack Pearl Harbor.[168]

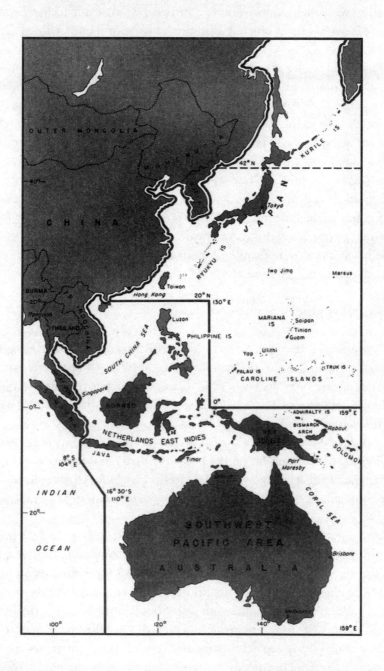

Pfennigwerth has made a point of informing his readers that *Betrayal at Pearl Harbor* has been severely criticised. He quotes one critic as follows:

> The noted writer on cryptanalysis, and the author of *The Codebreakers* – David Kahn – made the following reference to *Betrayal at Pearl Harbor* in an October 1991 article defending the work of the codebreakers in the lead-up to the Japanese attack: 'Aside from the fact that Churchill wanted the United States to fight Germany not Japan, the claim [that Churchill concealed foreknowledge of the attack from Roosevelt] is not only not substantiated by any documents (it is based chiefly on hypothesis and 'must have beens') but it is vitiated by technical errors ... it is improbable that the British ... would have limited exchanging code group recoveries with the Americans, when they would have benefited as much if not more than the Americans from learning as much as they could about the Japanese.'[169]

Pfennigwerth then commented:

> These are, in my view, perfectly fair criticisms of the book but as the reader will now realise, the hypotheses and 'must have beens' were not the work of Eric Nave. Its publication damaged his reputation and portrayed him as something of a crank ... It would have been better had his name been left off the title page ...
>
> As for Rusbridger, his journalistic sensation making with *Betrayal at Pearl Harbor* brought him more notoriety than fame, and precious little fortune. He died by his own hand on 16 February 1994 in allegedly bizarre circumstances, apparently unable to meet the demands of his creditors.[170]

Rusbridger was a charlatan, but he succeeded in beguiling a number of prominent people in Britain, America and Australia. One respected British historian, John Costello, even worked for a time as an adviser to Rusbridger and Nave. In his source notes to *Days of Infamy* Costello wrote, 'When the original British publisher bowed out after the government issued a 'D' notice to prevent Nave from publishing his memoir, the author of this book ceased to have any responsibility for either the manuscript or the conclusions of the work that finally appeared in 1990 [sic] under the title *Betrayal at Pearl Harbor*.'[171] Another of Costello's source notes refutes one of Rusbridger's more scurrilous claims. 'Mortimer's

1982 letter to the author does not state that Churchill (who was no longer prime minister when the war ended) had personally ordered the destruction [of the FECB records] as Rusbridger and Nave claimed in *Betrayal at Pearl Harbor.'*[172]

Ian Pfenningwerth and John Costello are among few serious scholars who have written extensively about the Far East Combined Bureau FECB. Neither, however, has examined the question of whether this arcane signals intelligence organisation could have detected the presence of the 22nd Air Flotilla on airfields around Saigon prior to 8 December. It is rather astounding that neither author seemed to comprehend the enormous threat this flotilla posed to *Prince of Wales* and *Repulse*.

By sending HMS *Prince of Wales* and HMS *Repulse* to the Far East Churchill had hoped to deter Japan from any new aggression that would lead to a war with Britain and America. While deterrence failed, the presence at Singapore of these two capital ships did cause Admiral Yamamoto to reinforce the 22nd Air Flotilla with 27 additional torpedo bombers. This has been well documented by historians Martin Middlebrook and Patrick Mahoney:

> The third step taken by the Japanese to protect the invasion convoys from *Prince of Wales* and *Repulse* was to reinforce the air units assigned to the area. Since there was no separate Japanese Air Force, an earlier plan had called for army planes to cover the landings. Yet the Japanese Navy had no confidence in the army to provide the necessary scale of air cover, and Admiral Yamamoto Commander-in-Chief of the Japanese Navy had ordered the 22nd Koku Sentai – the 22nd Air Flotilla – to move from its airfields in Formosa to Indo-China. Rear Admiral Sadaichi Matsunaga, the 22nd Flotilla's commander, had moved his headquarters to Saigon and his aircraft had followed … But, when the arrival of the two large British ships at Singapore became known, Admiral Yamamoto decided to strengthen this force by taking part of the Kanoya Air Corps away from the 21st Air Flotilla in Formosa. In this way, twenty-seven Mitsubishi Navy Type 1 G4MIS flew into Saigon just in time for the new war.[173]

The original date that the 22nd Air Flotilla – which consisted of almost 70 long-range bombers capable of carrying either bombs or torpedoes – arrived at airfields in southern French Indo-China cannot be pinpointed; however, it is believed to have been in late October. The reinforcements from Formosa arrived on 5 December.

Admiral Yamamoto's October order redeploying the 22nd Air Flotilla from Formosa to southern French Indo-China might well have been intercepted and read by FECB. What is virtually certain is that Admiral Phillips, Captain Leach and Captain Tennant never received any intelligence reports about the 22nd Air Flotilla, much less the reinforcements from the 21st Air Flotilla.

Leach clearly did not underestimate the threat that Japanese aircraft posed to his ship as well as to HMS *Repulse*. On the evening of 6 December he had spoken to his son, Henry, about the enormity of the odds they were up against. It can be assumed that he had discussed these concerns at length with his good friend, Bill Tennant, the *Repulse's* captain. Of the three senior officers in *Prince of Wales* and *Repulse*, Admiral Phillips was the most dismissive of Japanese airpower. He would not, however, have ignored any intelligence from FECB that the 22nd Air Flotilla had been redeployed and reinforced, and there would be records of his requesting information about the number of aircraft, their type, range and armament. He would not have gotten such precise information from FECB and in that climactic first week in December signals intelligence was no substitute for human intelligence out of French Indo-China.

One individual could have revealed much about the composition of the 22nd Air Flotilla to the British. He was Vice Admiral Jean Decoux, the 57-year-old Governor General of French Indo-China. It is all too easy for historians to dismiss Decoux as just another Vichy collaborator who was little more than a lackey of the Japanese. While he never declared himself for the 'Free French Movement' of the enigmatic Charles De Gaulle, Decoux was a substantial historical figure who had the courage to follow his convictions.

After July 1941, his position was unenviable. The Japanese Army had already occupied part of northern Indo-China and the Japanese Navy had established a forward naval base at Cam Rahn Bay. There were strong units of the Japanese Army and the Japanese Army Air Force in the south around Saigon and Japanese warships controlled the seas around the colony that stretched from the Chinese border in the north to the Thai border in the south.

Decoux could expect no reinforcements from Admiral Darlan as the latter's heavy ships at Toulon were short of fuel, but even if he had possessed an adequate supply of fuel, it would have availed him nothing because the Royal Navy controlled both ends of the Mediterranean. Admiral Darlan, therefore, could not send any warships to the Far East without the consent of the British. It was not only the overwhelming Japanese military presence that concerned Decoux. The Japanese using intimidation and coercion were systematically stripping his colony of its mineral resources and its rice crop, which at the time was the third largest in the world.

Notwithstanding the Japanese presence, Decoux controlled all French military forces in Indo-China and governed the native populations that consisted of the French protectorates of Cambodia, Laos, Annam, Tongkin and the colony of Cochin-China. His army numbered 80,000–100,000, but most of them were ill equipped native recruits; however, Decoux did have hardened troops of the French Foreign Legion under his command. His tiny air force had at least one squadron of Morane-Saulnier M.S. 406 fighter aircraft, and on 8 June 1940 one of these aircraft in the hands of a superb pilot shot down three Messerschmitt Bf 109s in fifteen seconds. The French Navy in Indo-China included the light cruiser *Lamotte-Picquet* armed with eight 6.1-inch guns in four turrets and two sloops, *Admiral Charner* and *Dumont D'Urville*, each armed with three 5.5-inch guns in three turrets. These sloops had been designed for tropical service with special arrangement for circulation of cool air.

Decoux's guiding principle was to use his military forces to assert French sovereignty over the entire colony; however, he knew that at any time the Japanese could arrest him and demand the surrender of his forces. In the event that his forces refused to surrender, he felt certain they would be annihilated. Why the Japanese did not disarm the French forces in Indo-China early on remains a mystery. It is conceivable that Japan thought Vichy France would eventually declare war on Britain and that Decoux' forces could be used to garrison Indo-China, thereby releasing Japanese troops for operations elsewhere.

Decoux insisted that the Japanese comply with their treaty obligations to compensate the French for everything that was exported to Japan including the vital rice crop. He resolved to defend the borders of French Indo-China from any aggression by Thailand, which later would become Japan's ally by declaring war on Britain and the US. At the same time Decoux wanted to safeguard some 40,000 Europeans, most of whom were French, and to protect the inhabitants of Indo-China from starvation. In mid September 1940, three months after France's surrender, Thailand demanded that France cede certain border territories together with some islands in the Mekong River. Decoux rejected this demand and took the drastic step of calling up French males throughout the colony between the ages of 40 and 50.

In January 1941 after Thai troops had crossed the border, Admiral Decoux ordered his naval units to sea. His small squadron led by the cruiser *Lamotte-Picquet* engaged and defeated most of the Thai fleet sinking or disabling two coast defence ships armed with four 8-inch guns. A few months later the Japanese intervened. Under the guise of mediation, Japan forced the French to cede all of the disputed territory to Thailand. These events did not go unnoticed by the American Secretary of State, Cordell Hull. On 6 April he told the British ambassador Lord Halifax that the government of Thailand had colluded with the Japanese to secure Tokyo's aid in their war with the Vichy French.

Notwithstanding this three-month war, Thailand ceased to pose any real threat to French Indo-China. The Empire of Japan was a different matter. Admiral Decoux and his superiors in Vichy well understood their grim choices: an undeclared war with Japan resulting in an overwhelming military defeat, abject surrender without resistance or an accommodation with Japan that would preserve the semblance of French rule.

On 19 July the axe fell. The Japanese envoy in Vichy delivered his government's ultimatum that Japan demanded the right to occupy all of French Indo-China with the provisos that France would retain sovereignty and that Admiral Decoux would continue to be Governor-General and the Commander-in-Chief of all French military forces. The Vichy government quickly acceded and within ten days the Japanese occupied southern French Indo-China including Saigon and its airfields, which placed Japanese aircraft within range of Singapore for the first time. From then until the outbreak of the war in the Pacific, Admiral Decoux and his staff had front row seats to the stage on which the Japanese were marshalling their military might for the most egregious act of aggression in their entire history.

In contrast, the British military in Singapore had little knowledge of what was happening in French Indo-China other than official announcements from Vichy and Tokyo. Their two most important channels of intelligence were the Free French organisation in Singapore and a secret channel with Admiral Decoux. The Free French organisation was headed by Monsieur Baron who was more successful at public relations than he was at acquiring military intelligence. The channel to Decoux seems to have been the brainchild of Admiral Sir Geoffrey Layton, Commander-in-Chief China, the highest ranking Royal Navy officer in the Far East. Although Decoux was well known to a number of Royal Navy officers with whom he had worked prior to the fall of France, it is unclear whether he and Admiral Layton ever met. Early in 1941, with permission of the Admiralty, Layton opened secret negotiation with Decoux. The story that was leaked to the press was that the Commander-in-Chief China offered economic aid to the French Governor-General in exchange for a pledge not to interfere with British shipping in the coastal waters of French Indo-China. The possibility that Decoux, who had only a handful of warships, might order them to interfere with British shipping seems preposterous. The possibility that Layton was trying to improve relations with Decoux in order to open a possible channel of military intelligence seems much more plausible.

By the autumn of 1941 Decoux's situation was becoming critical. The Japanese continued to demand the colony's mineral resources and most of its rice crop. For compensation the Japanese sometimes paid the French in a currency printed by the Japanese exclusively for use in French Indo-China. Since the currency had little real value, inflation threatened to destroy the economy, and with the forced export of rice, starvation loomed.

While Decoux like many other officers in the French Navy deeply resented the attack ordered by Churchill on French ships at Mers-el-Kébir where 1,000 French sailors perished on 3 July 1940, it seems doubtful that he was either pro-German or pro-Japanese. What has been largely overlooked is that in early 1941 Decoux and Admiral Layton commenced secret negotiations. The American war correspondent, Cecil Brown, had exceptionally good sources in Singapore and was keenly interested in what was happening in French Indo-China. His diary for 7 October 1941 reads in part:

My contact with the Free French finally bore fruit today. Dr. May and M. Baron, head of the Free French movement here, gave me a good story. They showed me secret documents they'd just gotten hold of revealing the extent of Vichy's collaboration with the Japanese ... At the moment

the Japanese are exerting all kinds of pressure on Vichy to surrender additional oil storage facilities and to permit Japanese control of the entire
postal system, telegraph and communication … the 'honor' with which
the Japanese carry on their business dealings is shown in their treatment
of the French in Indo-china. I saw a document showing that under two
treaties the entire coal production of Indo-China was reserved for Japan as
well as the entire output of iron, tin, manganese, chromium and antimony
… Under the treaty, payment by Japan was to be made in gold dollars
or in goods. After the agreement was made the Japanese informed the
Vichy authorities in Indo-China that their gold was frozen and that they
would pay with goods and raw materials … On September 18th, Decoux
was asked by a reporter of *Tokyo Nichi-Nichi* if he was satisfied with the
Franco-Japanese agreement. 'Until now,' Decoux said, 'Indo-China has
completely fulfilled all that was asked of her. She has sent everything that
Japan has requested and that we promised to send, but the Japanese have
not sent us the goods that they promised. We have difficulties getting
things we need from the Japanese, and we reserve our opinion on answer-
ing that question until the promised goods arrives [sic].'[174]

Seven weeks later Brown was able to get a story from Duff Cooper,
Churchill's representative in Singapore, that the latter should never have
revealed. Brown's diary for Friday 28 November reads:

Duff Cooper is still working on his report on the Far East. He was astonished to find that Admiral Sir Geoffrey Layton was carrying on diplomatic
relations with Indo-China. The story I get is this: Some time ago Layton
telegraphed the Admiralty that he didn't want to dissipate his forces and
the French in Indo-China had some naval units which could cause some
trouble and interfere with shipping. He therefore asked if he could nego-
tiate with Indo-China. He was told to go ahead. As a result he negotiated
with Admiral Decoux, the Governor-General in Indo-China, an accord
that if the French didn't interfere with shipping on the China coast or
infringe on British naval rights then certain raw materials, but not war
materials, would be sent to Indo-China.[175]

How much raw materials reached Indo-China is unclear. The real
import of what Cooper revealed to Brown is that Admiral Decoux had a
secret means of communicating with Admiral Layton.

The 22nd Air Flotilla and part of the 21st Air Flotilla with almost 100 naval aircraft capable of carrying either bombs or torpedoes were clearly prepared for action on 8 December. Their presence on airfields around Saigon would not have escaped the attention of the French. The deployment of an entire flotilla could not have been accomplished without some cooperation from Decoux's senior air force staff officers. While Decoux's air force was not large, nevertheless his aircraft would have made routine flights over the three airfields around Saigon and his pilots would have reported to him on the numbers and the types of aircraft they had seen from the air. It is highly probable that the Saigon police learned in late October that the commander of the 22nd Air Flotilla, Rear Admiral Matsunaga, had established his headquarters in Saigon. Admiral Decoux, whose headquarters were also in Saigon, could make reasonably accurate estimates of the Japanese naval air presence. Even if he had not had a naval background, Decoux very likely would have understood the threat that the 22nd Air Flotilla posed to *Prince of Wales* and *Repulse* in the event they were to venture into the Gulf of Siam.

Why did Decoux withhold this vital information from Admiral Sir Geoffrey Layton? This is indeed a troubling question. In the recent past Decoux had been involved with the Royal Navy and he had reason to loathe the Japanese. In September 1940 the Japanese Army had overrun a French Fort in Northern Indo-China and massacred the garrison; 800 French soldiers had perished. This happened despite the fact that a few days previously French officials had signed a treaty giving Japan the right to use certain airfields and port facilities in northern Indo-China.

Decoux might well have been tempted to tell Layton what he knew about the 22nd Air Flotilla; however, he did not. His primary loyalties lay with 'La Belle France' and the French Navy. He knew that if the Japanese learned that he had given Admiral Layton this vital information, they might have summarily executed him. The Japanese would have dismantled the entire French colonial administration and interned all French military forces including the hapless Governor-General. This would have ended French sovereignty in Indo-China, perhaps forever. It, however, seems probable that Decoux informed Admiral Darlan of the massive build-up of Japanese naval aircraft.

The British had obtained some French naval codes in early July 1940. On 1 July 1940 Admiral Darlan had ordered all French ships to return immediately to French ports. The French submarine *Narval* commanded by Capitaine de Corvette Drogou received the order in the Mediterranean and broadcast a reply that became symbolic of Free French resistance everywhere. '*Trahison sur toute la ligne, je rallie un port anglais.*' ('Betrayal all along the line, I am making for an English port.') A few days later *Narval* arrived at Grand Harbour, Malta. Capitaine Drogou promptly turned over the French naval codes to officers of the Royal Navy.

There is no historical evidence that FECB intercepted or read any signal from Decoux's headquarters in Saigon to Darlan's headquarters in France; however, that possibility cannot be entirely excluded in view of the probable destruction of all the FECB records for 1941. The monitoring stations on Stonecutter's Island and at the Singapore Naval Base certainly had the capacity to intercept a French naval signal coming from Saigon; however, it is probable that these two stations were too busy intercepting Japanese naval signals to bother with any French ones. Furthermore, although the British had acquired the French naval codes used by the submarine *Narval* in early July 1940, Admiral Darlan may have changed all his codes long before the 22nd Air Flotilla's appearance in southern French Indo-China.

The failure of British intelligence in the Far East is not easily explained. The biggest problem for historians is the lack of official records. British historians almost unanimously agree that the official records of the Far East Combined Bureau were probably destroyed after the Japanese surrender.

The private records of Admiral Jean Decoux and his official records as Governor-General were probably destroyed months prior to the Japanese surrender. Field Marshal Count Hisaichi Terauchi, who commanded all Japanese southern armies, had established headquarters in Saigon early in 1945. By then French Indo-China was his strongest bastion in south-east Asia. His army was still formidable and he had a secure land line of communication with China where Japan maintained armies totalling a million men.

Terauchi was determined to fight to the death against any American invasion that seemed likely to be launched from the Philippines, which General MacArthur's forces had largely liberated by the end of February. Terauchi was concerned about what Admiral Decoux would do in that event. In November 1942 Vichy French forces in French North Africa had initially resisted US and British landings, but by 1945 the Vichy government no longer existed. Although Decoux's native troops seem to have been largely demobilised, he still commanded up to 10,000 French soldiers and an unknown number of French Foreign Legion troops.

On 9 March 1945, Terauchi demanded that Decoux place his forces under Japanese command. When Decoux refused, he was arrested and the French garrisons were surrounded 'and in the fighting that followed about 1,700 French troops were killed or simply massacred.'[176] Before he received this ultimatum Admiral Decoux had probably already ordered the destruction of all sensitive records.

If the precise causes of these intelligence failures remain unknown, their consequences are apparent. Admiral Phillips, Captain Leach and Captain Tennant would have been able to devise a far better battle plan had they had accurate information about the 22nd Air Flotilla. War would come to Singapore all too soon. The individual who would have the forthcoming responsibility for the deployment of HMS *Prince of Wales* and HMS *Repulse* was Admiral Sir Tom Phillips. The Admiral did not know half of what he would be up against.

Chapter XIII

The Empire of Japan

Shortly before 0755, 7 December, 1941, on a quiet Sunday morning, Commander Logan Ramsey US Navy stood near a window of the Ford Island Command Center, Pearl Harbor, watching the colour guard prepare to hoist the Stars and Stripes. Ramsey was more than slightly alarmed. Earlier that morning before he had dressed he had received a report from the duty officer on Ford Island that one of their planes (Patrol Wing 2) had just sunk a submerged submarine one mile off the entrance to Pearl Harbor. Ramsey immediately called the duty officer for the Commander-in-Chief US Pacific Fleet, Admiral Husband E. Kimmel.

At about 0755 Ramsey heard the scream of a plane flying low over Ford Island. He was certain it was a US Navy plane but in fact it was a single-engine Japanese Navy dive bomber that the Americans would name 'Val'. At 0757 a large explosion emanated from the area of the Patrol Wing 2 hangers. Ramsey raced across the hall to the radio room and ordered every seaman on duty to send out the following message uncoded:

Air Raid, Pearl Harbor, This is no drill

Those eight words became the most famous signal in the history of the US Navy. In the next few minutes, the Japanese caught seven American battleships at their moorings, clustered near Ford Island. Five of the seven were sunk; the other two were damaged. The most devastating hit was to USS *Arizona*, the flagship of the First Battleship Division. Around 0800 a bomb penetrated her deck armour and caused her forward magazine to explode. Captain Franklin Van Valkenburg, *Arizona's* skipper, and over 1,000 of his sailors died within a matter of seconds.

The Marsman building in Manila housed the headquarters of the US Asiatic Fleet. At 0300 on 8 December (Manila time) a seaman radio operator picked up Ramsey's message to the entire US Navy. The seaman knew it was authentic because he recognised the technique of the sender who was an old friend. The duty officer, Lieutenant Colonel William T. Clement USMC was the first officer to be informed and he immediately telephoned Admiral Thomas C. Hart, Commander-in-Chief US Asiatic Fleet, who was asleep in the nearby Manila Hotel, 300 yards away.

Instead of reading the message over the phone, Clement said, 'Admiral, put some cold water on your face. I'm coming over with a message.'[177] Sitting on the edge of his bed Admiral Hart scrawled the following words for immediate dispatch to the US Asiatic Fleet:

Japan started hostilities.

Govern yourselves accordingly.

When Japanese bombs started exploding at Pearl Harbor it was a few minutes before 0200 Monday, 8 December in Singapore. At that moment Captain Leach was asleep in his sea cabin. Because Japanese convoys had been spotted by the RAF two days before heading toward Siam or Malaya, both *Prince of Wales* and *Repulse* were in a high state of readiness. It is likely that Leach slept in his uniform. Shortly before 0400 he was awakened and informed that a formation of hostile aircraft were approaching Singapore. He ordered his ship to action stations as 31 Japanese twin-engine Mitsubishi G4M1 'Betty' bombers approached Singapore Island at approximately 17,000 feet. The Japanese aircraft targeted civilian areas and two military airfields resulting in some 200 civilian casualties. Both *Prince of Wales* and *Repulse* opened fire with all of their anti-aircraft guns, but only *Prince of Wales'* twelve 5.25-inch guns could reach the raiders. None of the Japanese aircraft was shot down.

Moments later, at around 0415 Singapore time every ship in the Royal Navy received the following signal from the Admiralty:

Commence hostilities against Japan at once.

Soon after the air raid ended, Leach spoke over his ship's loudspeakers. He informed the ship's company that Japan had attacked both America and Britain and that both countries were now at war with Japan.

On this oppressively hot day Leach prepared his ship for her operational orders which he expected at any time. At 1230 Admiral Phillips summoned his senior officers to *Prince of Wales* to decide on a course of action for the two capital ships and their escort of destroyers. Those present included Captain Leach of *Prince of Wales*, Captain Tennant of *Repulse*, Rear Admiral Palliser, Phillips' chief of staff, and Captain L.H. Bell, Captain of the Fleet. In all probability, both Leach and Tennant were more realistic about their desperate situation than Admiral Phillips.

In all fairness, Phillips lacked thorough intelligence on the enemy air force of which there were two components, the Japanese Army Air Force and the Japanese Navy Air Force. Admiral Phillips believed that the enemy aircraft operating from airfields in French Indo-China were Japanese Army aircraft, which did not carry torpedoes. The news from Pearl Harbor seemed to confirm that Japanese aircraft carriers were not a threat. The air raids at Pearl Harbor were now over and it could be assumed that the Japanese carriers and their escorts were rapidly withdrawing toward Japanese home waters. This proved to be a correct assumption; however, the assumption that Japanese naval torpedo bombers did not operate from land bases in Indo-China would prove to be terribly wrong.

There are no minutes of that 1230 conference on 8 December, but Captain Bell was able to give the Admiralty his recollection of Admiral Phillips' thoughts that day:

He calculated that the Japanese aircraft would not be carrying antiship bombs and torpedoes, and his force would only have to deal with hastily organised bombers from Indo-China during its retirement.[178]

In the stifling heat of the Admiral's dining cabin Phillips made the fateful decision that *Prince of Wales* and *Repulse* with four destroyers, now designated Force Z, would attack Japanese transports off Kota Bharu in northern Malaya at first light on 10 December. There had been little discussion and neither Captain Leach nor Captain Tennant had dissented. It was obvious to both of them that Admiral Phillips was determined to undertake this mission.

Later that same afternoon Leach had some leisure time and he and Henry arranged to meet at the naval base swimming pool. Henry, not being a strong swimmer, merely splashed about to get cool while his father swam several lengths. After a short while father and son joined Bill Tennant, whom Henry had not met before. The three of them relaxed over gin slings, a meeting that would be forever etched in Henry's memory. Decades later, Admiral of the Fleet Sir Henry Leach described that scene:

> It was obvious that the two Captains were close friends and held each other in mutual respect. That they were under considerable strain at the prospect, which had all the ingredients of a one-way mission, was also not hard to discern for the talk was rather desultory – of trivialities and of home. We parted and two hours later Force Z sailed.[179]

Two war correspondents were invited to accompany Force Z, Cecil Brown and O'Dowd Gallagher, a South African with the *London Daily Express*. The arrangements were made at the last minute and in the resulting confusion both Brown and Gallagher were placed in the wrong ship, *Prince of Wales*, which had no extra cabins owing to the presence of Admiral Phillips and his staff. Instead of delegating the task of informing Brown and Gallagher that they would have to transfer to *Repulse*, Leach spoke to them himself. The two correspondents, who had been told that they would be in the flagship, were openly disappointed. Leach brushed aside their protests but handled them with such courtesy that Brown could not help but feel kindly toward him.

> Captain Leach stood at the top of the gangway and called to us: 'You will be very comfortable in the *Repulse* and they have made arrangements for you to have a good time.' 'Thank you, sir,' I called back. 'Take care of yourself.'[180]

Cecil Brown had no business going on a hazardous mission. He was 34 years old and suffered from periodic bouts of dengue fever. Since his arrival in Singapore, he had been involved in two serious accidents. On 6 November returning from a northern airbase in a South African-made Vildebeest, a torpedo bomber of ancient vintage, the pilot overshot the runway at Seletar airfield on Singapore Island. Brown's aircraft came to a stop with its nose pointing directly into the ground and the tail sticking straight up in the air. The wings were smashed and gasoline was spraying out of them. The pilot, the wireless operator and Brown extricated themselves with some difficulty and luckily all escaped serious injury. Four days later Brown and Gallagher with a group of other correspondents had gone to a small island off Singapore to watch 6-inch guns firing at night. Afterwards, the two of them scrambled into the back of an empty army truck which suddenly starting rolling down an embankment. A bench flew through the air and landed on Brown, injuring him rather painfully over his kidneys.

Repulse had steamed out into the Straits of Johore ahead of *Prince of Wales*. Brown described the scene as *Prince of Wales* took her position ahead of *Repulse*.

> It was a beautiful evening, that twilight of Monday, December 8th. The bright-red sunset silhouetted the palms on the shore. Within minutes the *Prince of Wales* drew up alongside and passed us. The crews of each ship stood at attention. Captain William Tennant on our bridge waved his white hat. Two men standing on the bridge of the *Prince of Wales* waved their hats. They were Admiral Tom Phillips and Captain Leach.[181]

Cecil Brown's diaries, entitled *Suez to Singapore,* were published in 1942. There were at least four printings but today they are largely unknown, yet Brown's book possesses a distinction that no other book has. It has a claim to being the best firsthand account of the final action of *Prince of Wales* and *Repulse*. 90 out of 110 officers in *Prince of Wales* were saved. It is surprising that none of those who survived the war published a full-scale account of this battle until Geoffrey Brooke published *Alarm Starboard!* in 1982.

Brown's station was the flagdeck of *Repulse*. Until the very end he was able to observe *Prince of Wales* from a distance of less than half a mile and he watched the swarms of Japanese aircraft that assailed both ships. Most signals from Admiral Phillips to Captain Tennant were sent by signal lamps and it was the duty of the flagdeck yeoman in *Repulse* to receive and record these signals. Shortly after their receipt these signals were posted on the notice board of the wardroom; despite the distraction of being under repeated air attacks, Brown immediately recorded these and everything else he saw and heard. Most of what he wrote in his diaries had to do with *Repulse*, but some entries quote Admiral Phillips' signals from *Prince of Wales*.

For most of Tuesday 9 December *Prince of Wales* and *Repulse* had the benefit of thick, low clouds and they were not spotted by any Japanese aircraft. Brown suffered intensely from the unrelenting heat and humidity that prevented him from sleeping. The high point of that day for Brown was hearing President Roosevelt speak of 'a date that will live in infamy'. Brown's diary's words reflected his emotion:

> At 7:30 this morning we sat in the wardroom at breakfast. Over the radio we heard President Roosevelt speak to Congress putting the United States in a state of war with Japan.
>
> I had never felt what I felt at that moment. I wanted to get up and give a toast with my water glass and jump on the table and shout. It was strange. None of the officers in the wardroom said anything, and since they showed no reaction I decided against being ostentatious.[182]

In the afternoon Brown slept for an hour and then came up to the wardroom for tea about 1530. He was told that if they had already been spotted, the expectation was that there would be a destroyer or cruiser attack at dusk. He was assured that tomorrow would be filled with action.

Shortly after tea Admiral Phillips made the most important announcement of the day by a signal to all ships in the squadron. The news was not good.

> The enemy has made several landings on the north coast of Malaya and has made local progress. Our army is not large and it is hard-pressed in places. Our air forces have had to destroy or abandon one or more airfields.
>
> Meanwhile, fast transports lie off the coast. This is our opportunity before the enemy can establish himself. We have made a wide circuit to avoid air reconnaissance and hope to surprise the enemy shortly after sunrise tomorrow, Wednesday. We may have the luck to try our mettle

against some Japanese cruisers or some destroyers in the Gulf of Siam. We are sure to get some useful practice with high-angle armament, but whatever we meet I want to finish quickly and so get well clear to the eastward before the Japanese can mass too formidable a scale of air attack against us. So shoot to sink.[183]

This message gave officers and ratings little encouragement. The British Army and the RAF in northern Malay had not been able to prevent the initial Japanese landings. Phillips' message was not particularly sanguine about surprising the enemy shortly before dawn. The emphasis was on finishing quickly and getting well clear of Japanese air space.

About 1720 there was a break in the clouds and Force Z was spotted by a Japanese seaplane soon to be joined by two more aircraft of the same type. With no hope of surprise Admiral Phillips wisely decided to abandon the operation. At 2100, after almost two hours of darkness, *Prince of Wales* and *Repulse*, together with their destroyers, turned back towards Singapore. Phillips certainly consulted with Leach about this decision; while they were both disappointed, they agreed that without surprise their mission was virtually impossible.

Captain Tennant's announcement to the ship's company of their return to Singapore caused consternation. In the wardroom Cecil Brown found the officers sitting in chairs and divans in front of the fireplace with long faces. One of them was the *Repulse*'s executive officer Commander R.J.R. Dendy who the day before had welcomed Brown to the wardroom and had introduced him to each of the officers. In his diary that night Brown had described Dendy as someone 'middle-aged but boyishly husky who was tough and amiable.'[184]

The decision to return to Singapore disturbed Dendy, but he recognised that it was the right course of action. Dendy and Brown discussed the situation on one of the wardroom's divans. Dendy explained that surprise was essential to their mission and that they no longer had that advantage because they had been spotted by Japanese aircraft just before dusk. He then added, 'We don't know the extent or nature of the Jap air force or what we would run into. It isn't worth risking two capital ships under the strategic circumstances.'[185] In one revealing moment Dendy had admitted the abject failure of the code breakers at Far East Combined Bureau and the lack of human intelligence from French Indo-China.

Around 2245 on 9 December Admiral Phillips received the following message from his chief of staff, Rear Admiral Palliser at Singapore:

Immediate
Enemy reported landing Kuantan, latitude 03° 50′ North[186]

Some time in the early hours of 10 December Phillips ordered Force Z to proceed at high speed to Kuantan and engage any enemy ships in that area. There is no record of how Captain Leach felt about this new operation. Both the signal from Palliser to Phillips and the latter's abrupt decision to steam toward Kuantan remain controversial. Palliser's signal was deficient in two respects. It did not say whether the report of enemy landings was a confirmed or unconfirmed report and it gave no indication of the degree of its reliability. Admiral Phillips, who was well aware that the clouds had lifted and the morrow would likely bring clear skies, did not break radio silence and request fighter cover over Kuantan. It was well within the range of RAF fighter aircraft at Singapore.

The next day was bright and clear. Brown was captivated by the beauty and power of *Prince of Wales*:

This is a beautiful sight in the brilliant sunlight. I just took a picture of the *Prince of Wales* on the starboard beam. What power there is out here today! The *Wales* is moving with such rhythm, pushing a white wave away from her bow on each side. Every now and then she slaps the water and the spray comes racing over her forward deck. Our white ensign and hers, too, are rippling out in the breeze.[187]

Admiral Phillips found no enemy surface units off the coast of Kuantan and no indication of any enemy landings. Some time shortly after 1000 Phillips at last recognised his terrible peril and ordered Force Z towards Singapore. His luck was running out. Around 1020 lookouts sighted a single Nell bomber that was obviously searching for Force Z. The hour of the sighting was important because there was still time, just barely, for RAF fighter aircraft to provide cover for the two heavy units before Japanese Navy aircraft could deliver a devastating attack. Admiral Phillips still refused to break radio silence. It was an appalling decision.

At around 1115 on the flagdeck of *Repulse* Brown watched with grim fascination as nine high altitude bombers approached *Repulse* at what he estimated to be 12,000 feet. They were flying line astern coming towards the bow of *Repulse*.

> The guns of *Prince of Wales* just let go. At the same instant I saw the flame belching from the guns of the *Wales*, ours break into a chattering, ear-splitting roar. The nine Japanese aircraft are stretched out across the bright blue, cloudless sky like star sapphires of a necklace.[188]

Within two minutes the Japanese bombers engulfed *Repulse* in huge geysers of water. One bomb was a direct hit. It penetrated the catapult deck before exploding underneath in the Marines' mess, killing scores of Royal Marines. By 1123 the high altitude bombers had vanished. At 1140 Brown records, 'The *Prince of Wales* seems to be hit. She's reduced her speed ...'[189] In fact *Prince of Wales* was still undamaged.

The next attack on Force Z developed suddenly. It was carried out by as many as sixteen Mitsubishi G3M2 later given the code name 'Nell' by the Allies. It was one of the largest torpedo planes in the world with a wing span of 82 feet and a length of 53 feet 11 inches. Its two radial, air-cooled engines of 1075hp each gave it a maximum speed of 232mph. It carried a crew of seven, three of whom operated machine guns and one cannon. It had been developed in 1933 under the personal supervision of Admiral Isoroku Yamamoto when he was director of the technical division of the Air Office of the Imperial Navy, who had foreseen the need for a long range, land-based torpedo bomber. Yamamoto has been called 'Japan's greatest naval strategist and Commander'.[190] What made Yamamoto's aircraft so deadly was its long lance oxygen-propelled torpedo, which weighed 1764lbs.

At this stage of the battle, the officers known to be on *Prince of Wales'* compass platform, just above the admiral's bridge, were the Commander-in-Chief Admiral Phillips; the commanding officer, Captain Leach; Captain Bell of Admiral Phillips' staff; the navigating officer, Lieutenant Commander Rowell and the torpedo officer, Lieutenant Commander Harland. Since *Prince of Wales* had no torpedo tubes, Harland's principal duty was to ensure that *Prince of Wales'* electrical system worked properly. Harland was standing near Admiral Phillips just moments before the Japanese pilots dropped their torpedoes. A brief conversation between Harland and Phillips has been described as follows:

An officer on the bridge of the *Prince of Wales*, Lieutenant Commander R.F. Harland watched the aircraft approach and remarked, 'I think they are going to do a torpedo attack.' Admiral Phillips heard the remark and said something like, 'No, they're not. There are no torpedo aircraft about.'[191]

At least half of the sixteen Nells launched their torpedoes at *Prince of Wales*, two of which found their target. One torpedo hit the port side abreast of P3 and P4 turrets. Simultaneously, another hit the port side below Y turret that mounted four of her 14-inch guns. The latter torpedo not only blew a hole twelve feet in circumference in the hull but also knocked out both port propeller shafts. Immediately there was a violent shudder throughout the whole ship. Although *Prince of Wales* would absorb at least four additional torpedoes, she was probably doomed after that hit.

In *Repulse* Brown recorded that the first torpedo attack ended at 1151. Captain Tennant by a combination of skill and luck had managed to comb the torpedo tracks and avoid any additional damage to *Repulse*. Brown was exceptionally well informed on damage reports from *Prince of Wales*. At noon he learned of a signal from *Prince of Wales* that could not have been worse. 'We are out of control. Steering gear is gone.'[192] Historians agree that shortly afterwards Leach ordered two black balls to be hoisted at the yardarm indicating that his ship was out of control. Almost 45 minutes later Admiral Phillips sent a wireless signal to any British man-of-war. 'EMERGENCY. Send all available tugs. My position 003°40´N. 104°30´E.'[193] Nine minutes later he sent a second wireless signal with the same words except for his new location.

Phillips seemed to believe that *Prince of Wales* could be saved by tugs but it is extremely doubtful that Leach ever entertained such false hopes. It would have taken tugs from Singapore five or six hours to reach *Prince of Wales* and if by some miracle she was still afloat, she would have been a sitting duck for Japanese aircraft and submarines on the slow, tortuous inbound journey to Singapore. Indeed, Phillips' request for tugs was so bizarre that one must question his ability to make rational decisions.

The first news that the Naval Headquarters in Singapore had that *Prince of Wales* and *Repulse* were under attack from enemy aircraft came from Captain Tennant who broke wireless silence at 1158 after learning that Admiral Phillips had not yet requested air cover. The RAF scrambled eleven Buffalo fighter aircraft from the Sembawang Airfield under command of Flight Lieutenant Vigors, RAF. They arrived too late to save *Prince of Wales* and *Repulse*.

Shortly after 1220 Brown was thrown four feet across the flag deck when a torpedo struck 20 yards abaft his position. *Repulse* immediately began to list to port. Brown recorded the order over the loudspeaker, 'All possible men to starboard.'[194] *Repulse* was then struck by three torpedoes on the starboard side in quick succession. This 25-year-old battle cruiser was never designed to absorb that kind of punishment. Brown remembered Captain Tennant's last order over the loudspeaker.

All hands on deck. Prepare to abandon ship (pause). God be with you.[195]

The time was 1226. *Repulse* remained afloat for only another seven minutes.

Before Brown leaped into the sea wearing an airless life belt with his camera swinging wildly from his neck he glanced toward the *Prince of Wales* and later described what he had seen.

The torpedo-smashed *Prince of Wales*, still a half to three-quarters a mile ahead, is low in the water, half shrouded in smoke, a destroyer by her side.[196]

The destroyer was HMS *Express* which had come alongside *Prince of Wales'* starboard quarter. Captain Leach ordered all wounded and non essential personnel transferred to *Express*. By 1310 *Prince of Wales* was swiftly settling and listing badly to port. At 1312 Captain Leach gave the order to don lifejackets and abandon ship. Moments later eleven RAF Buffaloes appeared flying at a low altitude. At approximately 1320 HMS *Prince of Wales*, the flagship of Force Z, the next to newest battleship in the Royal Navy, capsized. Brown later wrote, '…And then I watched *Prince of Wales* go down, a big, dark thing sliding into nothingness.'[197]

The destroyer, HMS *Electra*, was a mile away, stationary in the calm sea, her Captain seemingly oblivious to the risk of being torpedoed. She had rescued 1,100 British soldiers from the hell of Dunkirk and now she proceeded to rescue hundreds of sailors and Royal Marines from *Repulse*. She also rescued the American journalist, Cecil Brown.

Brown had been in Singapore for over four months, but he had experienced little contact with the Royal Navy until the arrival of *Prince of*

Wales and *Repulse*. Brown quickly acquired a high regard for both ships which he felt were first class and he particularly liked their captains. Surprisingly, he had spent more time with Leach than with Tennant. On Wednesday 3 December Brown with other correspondents had been given a tour of the *Prince of Wales* by Leach and several days later he had had a long interview with him during which the Captain made a fine impression on the American. Their last conversation was by the gangway of *Prince of Wales* in the late afternoon of Monday 8 December.

Brown's only private conversation with Captain Tennant took place at sea on 9 December during the lull before the storm. At 0945 on 9 December Lieutenant Halton of the Royal Marines was told to bring Brown and Gallagher to the bridge. They had not met Captain Tennant before. He greeted Brown warmly saying, 'I am very glad to have an American reporter on board.'[198] Brown described Tennant as 'about fifty years old with an open, pleasant face, pinkish smooth skin with wrinkles around the eyes'.[199] During the interview Tennant paced up and down

The Hoe War Memorial in Plymouth displays the name of Captain Leach, his Executive Officer Commander Lawson and Admiral Sir Tom Phillips, all of whom lost their lives in *HMS Prince of Wales*. *(Courtesy of Adrian Marsden)*

his sea cabin, only twelve feet long and five feet wide, peering out of a scuttle (porthole) on each side and the window in front. By 1000 Brown and Gallagher were back in the wardroom with an off duty lieutenant. He never again spoke to Captain Tennant on board *Repulse*.

HMS *Electra* reached Singapore Naval Base 30 minutes after midnight with survivors from *Repulse* including Brown. Later Brown found a Lieutenant Commander from *Prince of Wales* who knew that Captain Leach had not survived. Regrettably Brown failed to get the officer's name. *Prince of Wales* had seven lieutenant commanders but the one whom Brown questioned was almost certainly Lieutenant Commander A.G. Skipwith, the First Lieutenant and third in command.

Brown was devastated by what Skipwith told him. He later wrote with understated poignancy:

I asked a lieutenant commander from the *Wales* about Admiral Phillips and Captain Leach. They were last seen standing on the bridge of the *Prince of Wales*. The Admiral and the Captain stood there together, the officer says, 'They would not go. As we started away, Captain Leach wayed, and called out, "Good-bye, Thank you. Good luck. God bless you".'[200]

Later that night Skipwith had to inform Henry Leach about his father. Henry had been wandering anxiously along the jetties where the destroyers had dropped off the survivors but none had been able to give him any news. Finally he trudged a mile and a half to the officers' quarters at the Fleet Shore Accommodation. There he encountered Skipwith who gave him the tragic news. Afterwards they stood looking at each other blankly. There was something more that Skipwith wanted to say. 'I'm very ... sorry,' he said chokingly. 'He was ... a fine man ... and we all loved him.'[201] Henry Leach nodded blindly and murmured, 'So did I.'[202]

Around 0500 on 11 December Brown finally got his story of the sinking of *Repulse* and *Prince of Wales* off by cable from Singapore to Manila from where it was relayed to New York. Before then few Americans knew of a Royal Navy Captain called John C. Leach. Now Brown told his fellow countrymen about *Prince of Wales*' commander.

Later, the ship was under water. Phillips and Leach were the last from the *Wales* to go over the side and they slid into the water together. It's probable that their reluctance to leave the ship until all possible men had left meant their deaths, since it's most likely they were drawn down by the suction when the *Wales* was on her side and then settled at her stern with her bow rising into the air … I did not meet Phillips but last week when I visited the *Wales* at the naval base, I had a long talk with Captain Leach. He's a jovial, convivial, smiling officer who gave me the impression of the greatest kindliness and ability.[203]

The news of the loss of *Prince of Wales* and *Repulse* sent waves of shock and grief throughout Britain. Outside the families of the ships' companies, none was more anguished than King George VI. He was touring Wales on 10 December (11 December in Singapore) when he was informed. According to his official biographer, Sir John Wheeler-Bennett, 'the King gave no sign to those about him of the shock which he had suffered.'[204] That night the King wrote in his diary:

> Just before leaving Bargoed I was told that both the 'P of W' & the 'Repulse' had been sunk by an air attack off the Malayan coast. This came as a very real shock, knowing what their loss means to us in those waters. We cannot spare any ships to replace them.[205]

That same day from the royal train the King wrote to Churchill:

> The news of the loss of the 'Prince of Wales' & the 'Repulse' came as a great shock to the queen and me when we were on our tour in S. Wales to-day. For all of us it is a national disaster, & I fear will create consternation in Australia. The lack of detail makes the fact harder to bear, coming on top of yesterday's bad news re the US battleships. I thought I was getting immune to hearing bad news, but this has affected me deeply as I am sure it has you …[206]

He could not have known that day that Captain Leach was missing, but he learned soon enough. These two Naval officers, both of whom had passed out from Dartmouth, had first met almost fifteen years before on the 1927 Royal Tour that took them around the world together in HMS *Renown*. Earlier in the year King George VI had inspected *Prince of Wales* at Rosyth after which the Captain and his King had enjoyed a drink together. There can be no doubt that this King grieved for this Captain.

In the first two days of hostilities the Empire of Japan, in sudden swift attacks, crippled the US Pacific Fleet at Pearl Harbor, destroyed most of the US Army Air Force's B-17s at Clark Field near Manila and sank HMS *Prince of Wales* and HMS *Repulse* off the coast of Malaya. None of these disasters was inevitable. If on 7 December the radar station on the north coast of Oahu had been under the command of a more competent officer, then the headquarters of the US Army and Navy in Honolulu could have had timely warning of the approach of large numbers of hostile aircraft and Pearl Harbor could have been an American victory, or at least a less damaging defeat. If on 8 December General Douglas MacArthur and his air force commander, Major General Lewis H. Brereton, had moved their aircraft out of harm's way, the B-17s would have been available for counterattacks on Japanese air fields in Formosa and in French Indo-China including the bases of the Japanese 22nd Air Flotilla. If tactical errors had not occurred on 10 December 1941, it is possible that both *Prince of Wales* and *Repulse* would have survived to fight another day.

Prince of Wales and *Repulse* might have been saved except for two tactical blunders. Admiral Phillips' chief of staff, Rear Admiral A.F.E. Palliser, had remained at the Singapore Naval Base. It was his duty to provide Admiral Phillips with accurate information about enemy movements. From 1730 on 8 December when Force Z, Phillips' squadron, headed out to sea, Admiral Palliser was presumably continuously on duty with little or no rest. Shortly before midnight on 9 December Palliser received a report from Army sources that the Japanese were landing at Kuantan not quite half the distance between Singapore and Kota Bharu. Palliser knew that this report had not been confirmed by either the Royal Air Force or the Royal Navy and he could have waited for confirmation or at least given some type of evaluation as to the report's reliability. It was a serious error by Palliser.

Except for that one signal Phillips would almost certainly have continued at high speed for Singapore and would have had almost six more hours of darkness before he would have been sighted by Japanese reconnaissance aircraft. Before the enemy could have mounted air attacks, Phillips would have had RAF fighter aircraft overhead.

Admiral Phillips' failure to signal Singapore that he urgently needed air cover was the most egregious error during the entire action. At approximately 1015 on 10 December a lookout had sighted a Japanese reconnaissance aircraft. The main Japanese attack did not develop for almost an hour, which was just enough time for RAF fighters to reach *Prince of Wales* and *Repulse*. But could the RAF and the RAAF have made a difference?

It is possible to compare the quantity and the quality of the Japanese Navy Air Force with the aircraft of the Royal Air Force and the Royal Australian Air Force. On 8 December the Japanese Navy had stationed its 22nd Air Flotilla on three airfields around Saigon in southern French Indo-China. This Flotilla's bomber and torpedo aircraft consisted of the following:

Genzan Kokutai – 36 G3Ms at Saigon
Mihoro Kolutai – 36 G3Ms at Thu Dau Moi
Kanoya Kolutai – 27 G4Ms at Thu Dau Moi

The Japanese principal torpedo aircraft was the G3M. Its main weaknesses were its relatively slow maximum speed of 232mph, its rear 20mm gun with a limited field of fire and its non-selfsealing gasoline tank that made it vulnerable to incendiary bullets.

On 8 December the British had the following squadrons of fighter aircraft based on Singapore Island:

243 Squadron   15 Buffaloes at Kallang under Sqn Ldr F.J. Howell
453 Squadron   18 Buffaloes at Sembewang under Flt Lt T.A. Vigors
488 Squadron   17 Buffaloes at Kallang under Sqn Ldr W.G. Clouston
4PRU   2 Buffaloes at Kallang under Sqn Ldr C.R.G. Lewis

The Buffalo, which was designated as the Brewster F2A-3 Buffalo by the US Navy, was a single-engine fighter with a radial air-cooled engine. It had a wingspan of 35 feet, a length of 26 feet 4 inches and its maximum speed was 321mph. Its armament consisted of four machine guns, all of which fired forward. The Americans only used the Buffalo in battle once, in the Battle of Midway, when a squadron of Marine Corps Buffaloes based on Midway Island attempted to intercept an approaching formation of 108 Japanese carrier aircraft. The American aircraft were pounced on by Mitsubishi A6M Reisen aircraft – better known as 'Zeros' – and most of the Marine fighter pilots were killed. RAF pilots would have called it 'a bloody shambles'.

Nevertheless, the Buffalo was more than a match for the Nell (Mitsubishi G3M), being approximately 100mph faster. In an attack from the rear or the side the Buffalo could fire four guns simultaneously while the Nell could only bear two guns at most on an attacking fighter. The Buffalo had one other significant advantage: it could absorb much more punishment than the Nell. At the time that Admiral Phillips should have requested air cover, Air Vice-Marshal Pulford had 11 Buffaloes sitting on the runway at Sembawang ready to scramble. At the beginning of hostilities he had 41 additional Buffaloes at his disposal. In the first two days of the war Pulford's fighter squadrons had incurred some losses, but most of his aircraft were still operational. The Air Vice Marshal would have committed every available aircraft to this battle had he known what was happening.

One can only speculate on the numbers of Nells and Bettys that could have been destroyed by the Buffalos, but their intervention could only have increased the odds in favour of *Prince of Wales* and *Repulse*. Flight Lieutenant T.A. Vigors in command of 453 Squadron deserves the last word.

> I reckon this must have been the last battle in which the Navy reckoned they could get along without the R.A.F. A pretty damned costly way of learning.
>
> I had worked out a plan with the liaison officer on the *Prince of Wales* by which I could keep six aircraft over him all daylight hours within 60 miles of the east coast to a point north of Kota Bharu. This plan was turned down by Admiral Phillips. Had I been allowed to put it into effect, I am sure the ships would not have been sunk. Six fighters could have made one hell of a mess of even 50 or 60 slow and unescorted torpedo-bombers.[207]

It is essential, at this point, to turn back to the final tragic moments on board *Prince of Wales*. Before she sank Admiral Phillips had ample opportunity to transfer his flag, as Commander-in-Chief of Force Z, from the sinking *Prince of Wales* to the destroyer *Express,* which was undamaged and totally operational and nothing in the traditions of the Royal Navy should have inhibited him from doing so. It is conceivable that Admiral Phillips, at the end, was no longer capable of making rational decisions. It is even more conceivable that he felt he could no longer live with himself and therefore decided to go down with his ship. In any event his failure to transfer his flag had profound consequences.

Once Captain Leach had done everything he could for his men and his ship, he could have been expected to save himself, but he did not choose to do so. Minutes before he had faced the hardest decision that any Captain has to face, the decision to abandon ship; now he had to decide whether it was his duty to stand by Admiral Phillips's side, knowing full well that by doing so he would lose his own life. His devotion to his duty as a Royal Navy officer controlled that final decision.

AFTERWORD

The death of Captain Leach became known throughout the Royal Navy soon after 10 December; nevertheless, naval procedures required a formal investigation with a report to the Admiralty before that body could officially notify Evelyn Leach.

The sad duty to send the official notification to her rested with Sir Henry V. Markham, the Permanent Secretary to the Lords, Commissioners of the Admiralty. Sir Henry's words revealed both his kindness and his grief. It was addressed to Mrs E.B. Leach, Yarner, Bovey Tracey, S. Devon.

29 January, 1942

Madam,

I am commanded by my Lords, Commissioners of the Admiralty, to inform you with reference to the Admiralty letter of 15 December, 1941, that your husband, Captain John Catterell Leach, M.V.O. D.S.O., Royal Navy is now known to have lost his life on 10 December, 1941, when H.M.S. *Prince of Wales,* of which he was in command, was sunk by enemy action.

My Lords desire me to convey to you their profound sorrow that these weeks of anxiety should have ended so unhappily and their deep sympathy in the great loss which you have sustained.

I am, Madam
Your obedient Servant
H.V. Markham[208]

On 6 April 1942 Mrs Leach received another Admiralty communication, a cover letter from the First Lord of the Admiralty, A.V. Alexander, MP.

It is with much pleasure that I send you the enclosed letter from the President of the United States ...[209]

The following letter was addressed to Mrs John C. Leach and was delivered by diplomatic pouch to the American Embassy in London from whence it went to Whitehall:

The White House
Washington
March 12, 1942

My dear Mrs Leach:—

Only a few days ago my son's destroyer came into port, after many miles of escort duty, and he has brought me a very wonderful medallion made for me on the *Prince of Wales* and sent to me by your husband, with a little note from him.

I want you to know how much I shall always appreciate this gift from him and from the ship's company of the *Prince of Wales*. Nor will I ever forget the privilege of meeting your gallant husband, and especially of attending divine service that day in Newfoundland last August when he read the lesson.

Nothing I can say will be of much help but I want you and your son to know that very many Americans have been thinking of you.

Very sincerely yours,
Franklin D. Roosevelt[210]

This letter was written 25 days after the fall of Singapore, one day after General MacArthur left Corregidor, and the same day that Dutch Forces formally surrendered the Netherland East Indies. The Empire of Japan seemed supreme throughout the Pacific. Yet the President of the United States found the time to write to the widow of a Royal Navy officer.

In May of that year, Mrs Leach received a confidential letter from the Central Chancery of the Orders of Knighthood, St. James's Palace, London. This letter began,

> Madam, I have the honour to inform you that your attendance is requested at Buckingham Palace at 10:15 o'clock a.m. on Tuesday, the 23rd June next, in order that you, as next of kin, may receive from the King the Insignia of a Companion of the Distinguished Service Order conferred on your husband the late Captain John C. Leach, Royal Navy, *H.M.S. Prince of Wales.*[211]

In August 1941 Leach had spent over ten days at sea with Prime Minister Churchill, the latter spending hours on the compass platform with the Captain of *Prince of Wales*. There is no record of their conversations, but there is the tribute that Churchill paid to Captain Leach in *The Grand Alliance, Volume III* of his famed work on the Second World War.

Many British readers will be acquainted with Midshipman Henry Leach's subsequent career in the Royal Navy. Many American readers will not be familiar with a career that took him to the highest rank in the Royal Navy.

In December 1943, Sir Henry was a 20-year-old lieutenant aboard the *Duke of York*. His action station was officer of the quarters of 'A' turret – four 14-inch guns each firing a shell of over ¾ ton to a range of 18 miles and each manned by 50 men. On Boxing Day, 26 December 1943, his turret helped to sink the formidable German battleship *Scharnhorst* in a stormy sea off the north cape of Norway.

Lieutenant Leach survived the war and chose to make the Royal Navy his life's work. He went on to command a destroyer, a squadron of frigates and a commando carrier before being promoted to flag rank. He has held the key appointments of Director of Naval Plans, Assistant Chief of Naval Staff and Vice Chief of the Defence Staff.

In April 1982, when Argentina suddenly invaded the Falkland Islands, Sir Henry was the First Sea Lord and the Chief of the

Naval Staff. The Royal Navy formed the vital component of the expedition to retake the Falkland Islands. Prime Minister Margaret Thatcher would later write of Sir Henry,

> When he [Leach] finally arrived, I asked him what we could do … Before this, I had been outraged and determined. Now my outrage and determination were matched by a sense of relief and confidence. Henry Leach had shown me that if it came to a fight the courage and profession-alism of Britain's armed forces would win through.[212]

On 21 April a self-assured Member of Parliament called Tam Dalyell had met privately with Prime Minister Thatcher to warn her of the danger that the Argentine Air Force posed to the Royal Navy. To make his point he had reminded her that HMS *Prince of Wales* and HMS *Repulse* were sunk by shore-based Japanese aircraft. The Prime Minister was undaunted. She replied, 'I know. One of my chief advisers is Admiral of the Fleet, Sir Henry Leach, the son of Captain Leach, who went down on the *Prince of Wales*.'[213]

Sir Henry now lives near Wonston, in Hampshire. On the long wall in Sir Henry's living room two photographs are predominant. One is a black and white photograph of his handsome father in the uniform of the Royal Navy with his ribbons and his four gold rings. The other is a colour photograph of the rust-covered hull of a great ship. It is HMS *Prince of Wales* in her final resting place off the coast of Malaya.

The *Prince of Wales* that Captain Leach commanded was the twelfth ship of the Royal Navy with that name. The original *Prince of Wales* had been commissioned in 1763 and Captain Leach's ship will not be the last. In 2008 the Ministry of Defence signed contracts to build the two largest aircraft carriers ever built for the Royal Navy. The second of these new aircraft carriers will be HMS *Prince of Wales*. She will be christened with an historic name and will have a heritage in which her future captains can take uncommon pride.

Appendix

HMS Prince of Wales

Class	King George V class
Builder	Cammell Laird and Company, Ltd
Ordered	29 July 1936
Laid down	1 January 1937
Launched	3 May 1939
Commissioned	19 January 1941 (completed 31 March)
Sunk	10 December 1941
Motto	'I serve'
Displacement	43,786 tons
Length	745 ft 1 in (overall)
	740 ft 1 in (waterline)
Beam	112 ft 5 in (max)
Draught	29 ft (mean standard)
	32 ft 6 in (mean deep)
Propulsion	8 Admiralty three-drum small-tube boilers with superheaters
	4 Parsons single-reduction geared turbines
	4 three-bladed propellers
	111,600 shp
Speed	28.0 knots (achieved 29.1 knots in service)

Range	3,100 nmi at 27 knots
	14,400 nmi at 10 knots
Complement	1,521 (1941)
Sensors and processing systems	Type 281 RADAR from January 1941
Armament (1941)	10 × 14 inch Mk VII guns
	16 × 5.25 inch dual purpose guns
	48 × 40 mm 2-pounder AA guns
	8 × 20 mm Oerlikon AA cannon

Armour

Main belt	14.7 in
lower belt	5.4 in
deck	up to 5.38 in
main turrets	12.75 in
barbettes	12.75 in

Aircraft carried	4 Supermarine Walrus seaplanes
	1 double-ended catapult

NOTES

Chapter I

1 Stephen Lacey, *Gardens of the National Trust* (London: National Trust Enterprises Limited, 1996) p. 79.
2 John Keegan, *The Price of Admiralty, The Evolution of Naval Warfare* (New York: The Penguin Group, 1990) p. XV.
3 *The New Encyclopaedia Britannica Micropoedia*, Volume III, 1975, p. 659.
4 Robert K. Massie, *Dreadnought-Britain Germany and the Coming of the Great War* (New York: The Random House Publishing Group, 1991) pp. 479–80.

Chapter II

5 John W. Wheeler-Bennett, *King George VI His Life and Reign* (London: The Reprint Society, 1959) p. 38.
6 Dr. Jane Harrold and Dr. Richard Porter, *Britannia Royal Naval College 1905–2005 A Century of Officer Training at Dartmouth* (Dartmouth, England: Richard Webb, Publisher, 2005) p. 33.
7 *Britannia Magazine*, Summer 1909, p. 184.
8 Ibid
9 *Britannia Magazine*, Summer 1910, p. 300.
10 Ibid
11 Letter from Dr. Jane E. Harrold to Douglas Hadler dated 25 July 2008.
12 Dr. Jane Harrold and Dr. Richard Porter, *Britannia Royal Naval College 1905–2005 A Century of Officer Training at Dartmouth*, cited supra, p. 144.
13 Robert K. Massie, *Dreadnought-Britain Germany and the Coming of the Great War* (New York: The Random House Publishing Group, 1991) p. 613.

14 Ibid, p. 748.

15 Ibid, pp.748–749.

16 Roy Jenkins, *Churchill A Biography* (New York: Farrar, Straus and Giroux, 2001) pp. 236–237.

17 John Keegan, *The Price of Admiralty The Evolution of Naval Warfare* (New York: The Penguin Group, 1990) p. 146.

18 ADM 196/56 Permanent Royal Navy Records of Captain John Catterall Leach, MVO DSO, the Public Record Office, Kew, Richmond, Surrey TW9 4DU.

19 Ibid

20 Ibid

21 John Keegan, *The Price of Admiralty The Evolution of Naval Warfare*, cited supra,p. 151.

Chapter III

22 Jane Marchand from her 1996 archaeological survey of Dartmoor for Dartmoor National Park Authority, Parke, Bovey Tracey, Newton Abbot, Devon TQ13 9JQ.

23 *The Bovey Book,* The story of a Devonshire town in words and pictures compiled by Veronica Kennedy (Bovey Tracey, Devon: The Bovey Tracey Heritage Trust, circa 2000) pp. 114–115.

24 Admiral of the Fleet Viscount Cunningham of Hyndhope, *A Sailor's Odyssey The Autobiography of Admiral of the Fleet Viscount Cunningham of Hyndhope K.T. G.C.B. O.M. D.S.O.* (New York: E.P. Dutton & Company, Inc., 1951) p. 121.

25 Admiral of the Fleet Sir Henry Leach, *Endure No Makeshifts Some Naval Recollections* (London: Leo Cooper an imprint of Pen & Sword Books Ltd., 1993) p. 1.

Chapter IV

26 Paul Johnson, *A History of the Modern World from 1917 to the 1980s* (London: Weidenfeld and Nicolson, 1983) p. 188.

27 John W. Wheeler-Bennett, *King George VI His Life and Reign* (London: The Reprint Society, 1959) f.n. p. 217.

28 Taylor Darbyshire, *The Royal Tour of the Duke and Duchess of York* (London: Edward Arnold & Co., 1927) pp. 300 and 302.

29 Permanent service record of Captain John C. Leach MVO DSO, Naval Historical Branch, Ministry of Defence, 24 Store, PP20, Main Road HM Naval Base, Portsmouth, Hants PO1 3 LU. (Obtained by Captain Leach's son, Admiral of the Fleet Sir Henry Leach, GCB, DL).

30 Ibid

31 Ibid

32 Ibid

33 Ibid

34 Admiral of the Fleet Viscount Cunningham of Hyndhope, *A Sailor's Odyssey The Autobiography of Admiral of the Fleet Viscount Cunningham of Hyndhope K.T. G.C.B. O.M. D.S.O.* (New York: E.P. Dutton & Company Inc., 1950) p. 578.

35 Samuel Eliot Morison, *The Rising Sun in the Pacific 1931–April 1942* (Boston: Little Brown and Company, 1948) p. 14.

36 Anthony Eden, Earl of Avon, *Facing the Dictators* (Boston: Houghton Mifflin Company, 1962) p. 606.

37 *The War Speeches of Winston S. Churchill Volume Three*, compiled by Charles Eade (Norwalk, Connecticut: The Easton Press, 2001) p. 418.

38 *The Neville Chamberlain Diary Letters Volume Four The Downing Street Years, 1934–1940*, edited by Robert Self (Aldershot: Ashgate Publishing Limited, 2005) p. 296.

39 *The Diaries of Sir Alexander Cadogan O.M. 1938–1945*, edited by David Dilks (New York: G.P. Putnam's Sons, 1972) p. 33.

40 Fleet Admiral William D. Leahy, *I Was There* (New York, London and Toronto: McGraw Hill Book Company, Inc., 1950) pp. 128–129.

41 Permanent service record of Captain John C. Leach MVO DSO, Naval Historical Branch, Ministry of Defence, 24 Store, PP20, Main Road HM Naval Base, Portsmouth, Hants PO1 3 LU. (Obtained by Captain Leach's son, Admiral of the Fleet Sir Henry Leach, GCB, DL).

Chapter V

42 Admiral of the Fleet Viscount Cunningham of Hyndhope, A Sailor's Odyssey The Autobiography of Admiral of the Fleet Viscount Cunningham of Hyndhope K.T. G.C.B. O.M. D.S.O. (New York: E.P. Dutton & Company, Inc., 1951) p. 199.

43 Winston S. Churchill, The Second World War Volume I The Gathering Storm (London: Cassell & Co. Ltd., 1948) pp. 125–126.

44 Ibid, p 553.

45 Ibid, p 554.

46 Stephen Roskill, Naval Policy Between the Wars II: The Period of Reluctant Rearmament 1930–1939 (St. James's Place, London: William Collins Sons & Co. Ltd., 1976) p. 333.

47 Permanent service record of Captain John C. Leach MVO DSO, Naval Historical Branch, Ministry of Defence, 24 Store, PP20, Main Road HM Naval Base, Portsmouth, Hants PO1 3LU. (Obtained by Captain Leach's son, Admiral of the Fleet Sir Henry Leach, GCB, DL).

48 V. E. Tarrant, King George V Class Battleships (London: Arms & Armor, a Cassell imprint, 1991) p. 35.

49 Ibid, p. 37.

Chapter VI

50 Admiral of the Fleet Viscount Cunningham of Hyndhope KT GCB OM DSO, *A Sailor's Odyssey* (New York: E.P. Dutton & Company, Inc., 1951) pp. 197–198.

51 Grand Admiral Raeder Supreme Commander of the German Navy 1928–1943, *Struggle for the Sea* (London: William Kember & Co. Limited, 1959) p. 124.

52 Ludovic Kennedy, *Pursuit The Chase and Sinking of the Bismarck* (New York: The Viking Press, Inc., 1974) pp. 19–20.

53 Paul Johnson, *A History of the Modern World from 1917 to the 1980s* (London: George Weidenfeld and Nicolson Ltd., 1983) p. 374.

54 Dan Van der Vat, *The Atlantic Campaign World War II's Great Struggle at Sea* (New York: Harper & Row, Publishers, 1988) pp. 163–164.

55 Ibid, p. 160.

56 Grand Admiral Raeder, *Struggle for the Sea*, cited supra, p. 203.

57 *The Oxford Companion to WW II*, General Editor I.C.B. Dear, (Oxford: Oxford University Press, 1995) p. 595.

58 Winston S. Churchill, *The Second World War ** Their Finest Hour* (London: Cassell & Co Ltd, 1949) p. 388.

59 Admiral of the Fleet Viscount Cunningham, *A Sailor's Odyssey*, cited supra, pp. 258–262.

60 Ibid, p. 262.

61 Correlli Barnett, *Engage the Enemy More Closely The Royal Navy in the Second World War* (New York: W.W. Norton & Company, 1991) p. 221.

62 Ibid, p. 245.

63 *The Oxford Companion to World War II*, cited supra, p. 1291.

64 Ibid

65 H. P. Willmott *The Great Crusade A New Complete History of the Second World War* (New York: Maxwell Macmillan International, 1989) p. 164.

66 Gordon W. Prange, *At Dawn We Slept The Untold Story of Pearl Harbor* (New York: Penguin Books USA Inc., 1982) p. 11.

67 Ibid, p. 9.

68 Ibid, pp. 16–17.

69 Ibid, p. 17.

70 *The Oxford Companion to World War II*, cited supra, p. 624.

71 Ibid

72 Lord Moran, *Churchill Taken from the Diaries of Lord Moran The Struggle for Survival 1940–1965* (Boston: Houghton Mifflin Company, 1966) p. 6.

Chapter VII

73 Duff Cooper, Viscount Norwich, *Old Men Forget The Autobiography of Duff Cooper* (London: Rupert Hart-Davis, 1955) p. 204.

74 Rt. Hon. Neville Chamberlain, M.P., *In Search of Peace* (New York: G.P. Putnam's sons, 1939) p. 143.

75 *The War Speeches of Winston S. Churchill Volume One*, compiled by Charles Eade (Norwalk, Connecticut: The Easton Press, 2001) p. 106.

76 Winston S. Churchill, *The Second World War Volume I The Gathering Storm* (London: Cassell & Co. Ltd., 1948) p. 320.

77 Ibid, p 552.

78 V.E. Tarrant, *King George V Class Battleships* (London: Arms and Armor, a Cassell Imprint, 1991) p. 22.

79 Ibid, p. 35.

80 Ibid, pp. 42–43.

81 H.V. Morton, *Atlantic Meeting* (New York: Dodd, Meade & Company, 1943) p. 39.

82 V.E. Tarrant, *King George V Class Battleships*, cited supra., p. 43.

Chapter VIII

83 Ludovic Kennedy, *Pursuit The Chase and Sinking of the Bismarck* (New York: The Viking Press, 1974) p. 23.

84 Jane's Fighting Ships, Founded in 1897 by Fred T. Jane (London: Sampson Low, Marston & Co. Ltd., 1940) p. 212.

85 Ludovic Kennedy, *Pursuit*, cited supra, p. 23.

86 Ibid, p. 29.

87 Ibid, p. 24.

88 Ibid, p. 38.

89 Ibid

90 Correlli Barnett, *Engage The Enemy More Closely The Royal Navy in the Second World War* (New York: W.W. Norton & Company, 1991) p. 292.

91 Ludovic Kennedy, *Pursuit*, cited supra, p. 43.

92 Captain Russell Grenfell RN, *The Bismarck Episode* (New York: The Macmillan Company, 1949) p. 42.

93 H.V. Morton, *Atlantic Meeting* (New York: Dodd, Meade & Company, 1943) pp. 73–74.

94 Captain Russell Grenfell RN, *The Bismarck Episode*, cited supra., p. 88.

95 Ibid

96 Ibid, p. 89.

97 Ludovic Kennedy, *Pursuit*, cited supra, p. 115.

98 Captain Russell Grenfell RN, *The Bismarck Episode*, cited supra, p.135.

99 Ibid

100 Correlli Barnett, *Engage the Enemy More Closely*, cited supra, p. 314.

101 Ludovic Kennedy, *Pursuit*, cited supra, p. 226.

102 Geoffrey Brooke, *Alarm Starboard! A Remarkable True Story of the War at Sea* (Barnsley, South Yorkshire: Pen & Sword Maritime, an imprint of Pen & Sword Books Ltd., 2004; first published in Great Britain in 1982 by Patrick Stephens) p. 73.

103 John W. Wheeler-Bennett, *King George VI – His Life and Reign* (London: The Reprint Society Ltd. 1959) pp. 293–4.

104 The Royal Archives, The Round Tower, Windsor Castle
105 Ibid
106 Geoffrey Brooke, *Alarm Starboard! A Remarkable True Story of the War at Sea*, cited supra, p. 76.

Chapter IX

107 Martin Gilbert, *Finest Hour Winston S. Churchill 1939–1941* (London: Heinemann-Minerva, an imprint of Octopus Publishing Group, 1989) p. 164.
108 John Colville, *The Fringes of Power 10 Downing Street Diaries 1939–1955* (New York London: W.W. Norton & Company, 1985) p. 736.
109 Matthew B. Wills, *Wartime Missions of Harry L. Hopkins* (Bloomington, Indiana: Authorhouse, 2004) p. 35.
110 Winston S. Churchill, *The Second World War Volume I The Gathering Storm* (London: Cassell & Co. Ltd., 1948) p. 558.
111 H.V. Morton, *Atlantic Meeting* (New York: Dodd, Meade & Company, 1943) p. 15.
112 Ibid, p. 17.
113 Ibid
114 Ibid, p. 26.
115 Ibid, pp. 27–28.
116 Ibid, p. 42.
117 Winston S. Churchill, *The Second World War Volume III The Grand Alliance* (London: Cassell & Co. Ltd., 1950) p. 381.
118 H.V. Morton, *Atlantic Meeting*, cited supra, pp. 96–97.
119 Ibid, pp. 109–110.
120 Ibid, p. 187.
121 Ibid, pp. 188–189.
122 Winston S. Churchill, *The Second World War Volume III The Grand Alliance*, cited supra, P. 390.
123 H.V. Morton, *Atlantic Meeting*, cited supra, p. 147.
124 The Public Record Office, Kew, Richmond, Surrey TW9 4DU.

Chapter X

125 Patrick Boniface, HMS *Cumberland A Classic British Cruiser in War and Peace* (Penzance: Periscope Publishing Ltd., 2006) p. 45.
126 Admiral of the Fleet Viscount Cunningham of Hyndhope KT GCB OM DSO, *A Sailor's Odyssey* (New York: E.P. Dutton & Company Inc., 1951) p. 466.
127 General of the Air Force H.H. Arnold, *Global Mission* (New York: Harper & Brothers, 1949) p. 251.
128 Ibid, p. 104.
129 Ibid, p. 105.

Chapter XI

130   *The Oxford Companion to World War II*, General Editor I.C.B. Dear (Oxford: Oxford University Press, 1995) p. 713.

131   Admiral of the Fleet Viscount Cunningham of Hyndhope K.T. G.C.B. O.M. D.S.O., *A Sailor's Odyssey* (New York: E.P. Dutton & Company Inc., 1951) p. 410.

132   *The World Almanac of World War II*, Edited by Brigadier Peter Young (New York: World Almanac, an imprint of Pharos Books, 1981) pp. 121–122.

133   Geoffrey Brooke, *Alarm Starboard! A Remarkable True Story of the War at Sea* (Barnsley, South Yorkshire: Pen & Sword Maritime, an imprint of Pen & Sword Books Ltd., 2004; first published in Great Britain in 1982 by Patrick Stephens) p. 89.

134   Reference CHAR 2/421 The Sir Winston Churchill Archive Trust, Churchill College, Cambridge.

135   Arthur J. Marder, *Old Friends, New Enemies The Royal Navy and The Imperial Japanese Navy Strategic Illusions, 1936–1941* (Oxford: Clarendon Press, 1981) p. 68.

136   John Colville, *The Fringes of Power 10 Downing Street Diaries 1939–1955* (New York London: W.W. Norton & Company, 1985) p. 134.

137   Ibid, p. 752.

138   General Lord Ismay, *The Memoirs of General Lord Ismay* (New York: The Viking Press, 1960) p. 240.

139   Copy of the original provided the author by Admiral of the Fleet Sir Henry Leach, GCB, DL.

140   Cecil Brown, *Suez to Singapore* (New York: Random House, 1942) p. 127.

141   Admiral of the Fleet Sir Henry Leach, *Endure No Makeshifts Some Naval Recollections* (London: Leo Cooper, 1993) p. 6.

142   Ibid, p. 5.

143   Cecil Brown, *Suez to Singapore*, cited supra, pp. 279–282.

144   Duff Cooper Viscount Norwich, *Old Men Forget* (London: Rupert Hart-Davis, 1955) p. 291.

145   Peter Elphick, *Far Eastern File The Intelligence War in the Far East* (London: Hodder and Stoughton Ltd., 1997) p. 324.

146   Admiral of the Fleet Sir Henry Leach, *Endure No Makeshifts*, cited supra, p. 7.

147   Ibid

148   Ibid

149   Ibid

Chapter XII

150   Lionel Wigmore, *The Japanese Thrust Australia in the War of 1939–1945* (Canberra Australian War Memorial, 1957) p. 82, f.n.

151   F.H. Hinsley, *British Intelligence in the Second World War* Volume One (London: Her Majesty's Stationery Office, 1979) p. 53, f.n.

152 Ibid, pp IX-X.

153 *The Oxford Companion to World War II*, General Editor I.C.B. Dear (Oxford: Oxford University Press, 1995) p. 346.

154 James Rusbridger and Eric Nave, *Betrayal at Pearl Harbor* (New York: Simon & Schuster, Inc., first Touchstone Edition, 1992) p. 138.

155 Ibid, p 5.

156 Ibid, p 10.

157 Ibid, p 12.

158 Ibid, p 173.

159 Correlli Barnett, *Engage the Enemy More Closely The Royal Navy in the Second World War* (New York: W.W. Norton & Company, 1991) p. 401.

160 James Rusbridger and Eric Nave, *Betrayal at Pearl Harbor*, cited supra, p. 77.

161 Ibid, p. 88.

162 Ibid, p. 137.

163 Ibid, p. 138.

164 Ibid

165 Ibid, p. 88.

166 Ian Pfennigwerth, *A Man of Intelligence The Life of Captain Eric Nave Australian Codebreaker Extraordinary* (New South Wales: Rosenberg Publishing Pty Ltd, 2006) p. 12.

167 Ibid, p. 137.

168 Ibid, p. 178.

169 Ibid, p. 273.

170 Ibid, pp. 273-74.

171 John Costello, *Days of Infamy* (New York: Pocket Books, a division of Simon & Schuster Inc., 1994) p. 421, s.n. 67.

172 Ibid, p. 421, s.n. 76.

173 Martin Middlebrook and Patrick Mahoney, *Battleship The Loss of the Prince of Wales and Repulse* (London: Allen Lane Penguin Books Ltd., 1977) pp. 83-84.

174 Cecil Brown, *Suez to Singapore* (New York: Random House Inc., 1942) pp. 219-20.

175 Ibid, pp. 269-70.

176 *The Oxford Companion to World War II*, cited supra, p. 418.

Chapter XIII

177 Samuel Eliot Morison, *The Rising Sun in the Pacific 1931–April 1942* (Boston: Little Brown and Company, 1948) p. 168.

178 Correlli Barnett, *Engage the Enemy More Closely The Royal Navy in the Second World War* (New York London: W.W. Norton & Company, 1991) p. 410.

179 Admiral of the Fleet Sir Henry Leach, *Endure No Makeshifts Some Naval Recollections* (London: Leo Cooper, 1993) p. 8.

180 Cecil Brown, *Suez to Singapore* (New York: Random House, 1942) pp. 296–297.

181 Ibid, p. 297.

182 Ibid, p. 299.

183 Ibid, p. 305.

184 Ibid, p. 297.

185 Ibid, p. 310.

186 Arthur Nicholson, *Hostage to Fortune Winston Churchill and the Loss of the Prince of Wales and Repulse* (Thrupp-Stroud-Gloucestershire: Sutton Publishing Limited, 205) p. 217.

187 Cecil Brown, *Suez to Singapore*, cited supra, p. 312.

188 Ibid, p. 315.

189 Ibid, p. 317.

190 *Routledge Who's Who in World War II* edited by John Keegan (London: Routledge, 1995) p. 178.

191 Arthur Nicholson, *Hostage to Fortune*, cited supra, p. 124.

192 Cecil Brown, *Suez to Singapore*, cited supra, p. 319.

193 Arthur Nicholson, *Hostage to Fortune*, cited supra, p. 220.

194 Cecil Brown, *Suez to Singapore*, cited supra, p. 321.

195 Ibid, p. 322.

196 Ibid, p. 324.

197 Ibid, p. 329.

198 Ibid, p. 300.

199 Ibid

200 Ibid, p. 335–336.

201 Admiral of the Fleet Sir Henry Leach, *Endure No Makeshifts*, cited supra, p. 10.

202 Ibid

203 *Reporting World War II Part One American Journalism 1938–1944* (New York: Literary Classics of the United States Inc., 1995) p. 265.

204 John W. Wheeler-Bennett, *King George VI His Life and Reign* (London: the Reprint Society, 1959) p. 533.

205 Ibid

206 Ibid

207 Christopher Shores and Brian Cull with Yasuho Izawa, *Bloody Shambles Volume One The Drift to War to the Fall of Singapore* (London: Grub Street, 1992) p. 125.

Afterword

208 A copy of the original was furnished to the author by Admiral of the Fleet Sir Henry Leach, GCB, DL.

209 Ibid

210 Ibid

211 Ibid

212 Margaret Thatcher, *The Downing Street Years* (London: Harper Collins, 1993) p. 179.

213 *Memories of the Falklands*, edited by Iain Dale (London: Politico's Publishing, 2002) p. 47.

BIBLIOGRAPHY

Angelucci, Enzo & Paolo Matricardi, *World War II Airplanes Volume 1* (Chicago, New York, San Francisco: Rand McNally & Company, 1976)

Angelucci, Enzo & Paolo Matricardi, *World War II Airplanes Volume 2* (Chicago, New York, San Francisco: Rand McNally & Company, 1976)

Barnett, Correlli, *Engage the Enemy More Closely – The Royal Navy in the Second World War* (New York, London: W.W. Norton & Company, 1991)

Boniface, Patrick, HMS *Cumberland A Classic British Cruiser in War and Peace* (Penzance: Periscope Publishing Ltd., 2006)

Bredin, Dee, *Java Assignment, The National Geographic Magazine*, January 1942, p. 89.

Brooke, Geoffrey, *Alarm Starboard A Remarkable True Story of the War at Sea* (Barnsley, South Yorkshire: Pen & Sword Maritime an imprint of Pen & Sword Books Ltd., 2004) First published in Great Britain in 1982 by Patrick Stephens.

Brown, Cecil, *Suez to Singapore* (New York: Random House, 1942)

Cadogan, Sir Alexander, edited by David Dilks, *The Diaries of Sir Alexander Cadogan, 1938–1945* (New York: G.P. Putnam's Sons, 1972)

Cant, Gilbert, *The War at Sea* (New York: The John Day Company, 1942)

Chamberlain, M.P., The Rt. Hon. Neville, *In Search of Peace* (New York: G.P. Putnam's Sons, 1939)

Chamberlain, M.P., The Rt. Hon. Neville, edited by Robert Self, *The Neville Chamberlain Diary Letters Volume 4 The Downing Street Years, 1934–1940* (Aldershot: Ashgate Publishing Limited, 2005)

Churchill, Winston S., *The Second World War Volume I The Gathering Storm* (London: Cassell & Co. Ltd., 1948)

Churchill, Winston S., *The Second World War Volume III The Grand Alliance* (London: Cassell & Co. Ltd., 1950)

Colville, John, *The Fringes of Power – 10 Downing Street Diaries 1939–1955* (New York, London: W.W. Norton & Company, 1985)

Costello, John, *The Pacific War* (New York: Perennial an Imprint of Harper Collins Publishers, 2002) (Originally published in New York by Rawson, Wade in 1981)

Costello, John, *Days of Infamy* (New York: Pocket Books, a division of Simon & Schuster Inc., 1994)

Cunningham, Admiral of the Fleet Viscount Cunningham of Hyndhope K.T. G.C.B. O.M. D.S.O., *A Sailor's Odyssey* (New York: E.P. Dutton & Company, Inc., 1951)

Dale, Iain (ed) *Memories of the Falklands* (London: Politico's Publishing, 2002)
Darbyshire, Taylor, *The Royal Tour of the Duke and Duchess of York* (London: Edward Arnold & Co., 1927)

Dear, I.C.B. (ed) *The Oxford Companion to World War II* (Oxford: Oxford University Press, 1995)

Eden, Anthony, Earl of Avon, *The Memoirs of Anthony Eden Facing the Dictators* (Boston: Houghton Mifflin Company, 1962)

Elphick, Peter, *Far Eastern File The Intelligence War in the Far East, 1930–1945* (London: Hadder & Stoughton, 1997)

Field, James A. Jr., *The Japanese at Leyte Gulf The Shō Operation* (Princeton: Princeton University Press, 1947)

Francillon, René J. *Japanese Aircraft of the Pacific War* (Annapolis, Maryland: the Naval Institute Press, 1970)

Franklin, Alan and Franklin, Gordon, *One Year of Life The Story of HMS Prince of Wales* (Edinburgh and London: William Blackwood & Sons Ltd., 1944)

Grenfell RN, Captain Russell, *The Bismarck Episode* (New York: The MacMillan Company, 1949)

Harrold, Dr. Jane and Porter, Dr. Richard, *Britannia Royal Naval College – 1905–2005 A Century of Officer Training at Dartmouth* (Dartmouth: Richard Webb Publisher, 2005)

Hinsley, F.H., *British Intelligence in the Second World War, Volume One* (London: Her Majesty's Stationery Office, 1979)

Ismay, General Lord, *The Memoirs of General Lord Ismay* (New York: The Viking Press, 1960)

Jenkins, Roy, *Churchill A Biography* (New York: Farrar, Straus and Giroux, 2001)

Johnson, Paul, *A History of the Modern World from 1917 to the 1980s* (London: Weidenfeld and Nicolson, 1983)

Keegan, John, *The Price of Admiralty The Evolution of Naval Warfare* (New York: Penguine Group Viking Penguine, a division of Penguin Books USA Inc., 1988)

Keegan, John (ed) *Routledge Who's Who in World War II* (London: Routledge, 1995)

Kennedy, Ludovic, *Pursuit The Chase and Sinking of the Battleship Bismarck* (New York: The Viking Press, 1974)

Kennedy, Veronica, *The Bovey Book The Story of a Devonshire Town in Words and Pictures*, compiled by Veronica Kennedy for the Bovey Tracey Heritage Trust.

Kimball, Warren F. (ed) *Churchill and Roosevelt The Complete Correspondence Vol. I Alliance Emerging October 1933 – November 1942* (Norwalk, Connecticut: The Easton Press, 1995)

Leach, Admiral of the Fleet Sir Henry, *Endure No Makeshifts Some Naval Recollections* (London: Leo Cooper, 1993)

Leahy, Fleet Admiral William D., *I Was There* (New York: Whittlesey House McGraw-Hill Book Company, Inc., 1950)

Lucas, Ian F., *The Royal Embassy – The Duke and Duchess of York's Tour in Australasia* (London: Methuen & Co. Ltd., 1927)

Marder, Arthur J., *Old Friends New Enemies – The Royal Navy and the Imperial Japanese Navy – Strategic Illusions 1936–1941* (Oxford: Oxford University Press, 1981)

Massie, Robert K., *Dreadnought Britain, Germany and the Coming of the Great War* (New York: Ballantine Books – The Random House Publishing Group, 1991)

McMurtrie AINA, Francis E. (ed) *Jane's Fighting Ships 1940.* (London: Sampson Low, Marston & Co. Ltd., 1941)

McMurtrie AINA, Francis E. (ed) *Jane's Fighting Ships 1941* (New York: The MacMillan Company, 1942)

Middlebrook, Martin and Mahoney, Patrick, *Battleship The Loss of the Prince of Wales and Repulse* (London: Allen Lane Penguin Books Ltd., 1977)

Morison, Samuel Eliot, *The Rising Sun in the Pacific 1931–April 1942* (Boston: Little, Brown and Company, 1988)

Moran, Lord, *Churchill Taken from the Diaries of Lord Moran The Struggle for Survival 1940–1965* (Boston: Houghton Mifflin Company, 1966)

Morton, H.V., *Atlantic Meeting* (New York: Dodd, Mead & Company, 1943)

Nicholson, Arthur, *Hostage to Fortune: Winston Churchill and the Loss of the Prince of Wales and Repulse* (Stroud, Gloucestershire: Sutton Publishing Ltd., 2005)

Pffenigwerth, Ian, *A Man of Intelligence The Life of Captain Eric Nave Australian Codebreaker Extraordinary* (Rosenberg Publishing Pty. Ltd., 2006)

Prange, Gordon W., *At Dawn We Slept: The Untold Story of Pearl Harbor* (New York: Penguine Group Viking Penguine, a division of Penguin Books USA Inc., 1982)

Raeder, Grand Admiral Supreme Commander of the German Navy 1928–1943 (London: William Kimber and Co. Limited, 1959)

Roskill, Stephen, *Churchill and the Admirals* (New York: William Morrow and Company Inc., 1978)

Roskill, Stephen, *Naval Policy between the Wars – the Period of Reluctant Rearmament 1930–1039* (London: Collins, 1976)

Rusbridger, James and Nave, Eric, *Betrayal at Pearl Harbor How Churchill Lured Roosevelt into World War II* (New York: Simon & Schuster, 1992)

Sherwood, Robert E., *Roosevelt and Hopkins An Intimate History* (New York: Harper & Brothers, 1948)

Shores, Christopher and Cull, Brian with Yasuho Izawa, *Bloody Shambles Volume One The Drift to War to the Fall of Singapore* (London: Grub Street, 1992)

Simpich, Frederick, *1940 Paradox in Hong Kong, The National Geographic Magazine,* April 1940, p. 531.

Simpich, Frederick, *Behind the News in Singapore, The National Geographic Magazine,* July 1940, p 83.

Tarrant, V.E., *King George V Class Battleships* (London: Arms and Armour A Cassell Imprint, 1999)

Thatcher, Margaret, *The Downing Street Years* (New York: Harper-Collins Publishers, Inc., 1993)

Van der Vat, Dan, *The Atlantic Campaign World War II's Great Struggle at Sea* (New York: Harper & Row, Publishers, 1988)

Wheeler-Bennett, John W., *King George VI – His Life and Reign* (London: The Reprint Society Ltd., 1959)

Willmott, H.P., *The Great Crusade A New Complete History of the Second World War* (New York: The Free Press, a division of Macmillian Inc., 1989)

Wills, Matthew B., *Wartime Missions of Harry L. Hopkins* (Bloomington, Indiana: Authorhouse, 2004)

Young, Brigadier Peter (ed) *The World Almanac of World War II* (World Almanac An imprint of Pharos Books, 1986)

Young, Peter and Lawford J.P. (eds) *History of the British Army* (New York: G.P. Puttnam's Sons, 1970)

1940 Britannica Book of the Year
1941 Britannica Book of the Year
The New Encyclopoedia Britannica Micropoedia Volume III.
Reporting World War II Part One American Journalism 1938–1944 (New York: Library
   Classics of the United States, Inc., 1995)

Unpublished Sources

Letter from Captain John C. Leach to Prime Minister Winston S. Churchill
   dated 10 September 1941. Courtesy of the Public Record Office.
Letter from Captain John C. Leach to Prime Minister Winston S. Churchill
   dated 16 October 1941. Courtesy of the Sir Winston Churchill Archive Trust,
   Churchill College, Cambridge University.
Letter from Captain John C. Leach to Field Marshal Sir John Dill dated 15
   November 1941. Courtesy of Admiral of the Fleet Sir Henry Leach, GCB, DL.
Letter from Sir Henry V. Markham to Mrs E.B. Leach dated 29 January 1942.
   Courtesy of Admiral of the Fleet Sir Henry Leach, GCB, DL.
Letter from President Franklin D. Roosevelt to Mrs John C. Leach dated 12 March
   1942. Courtesy of Admiral of the Fleet Sir Henry Leach, GCB, DL.
Letter from First Lord of the Admiralty, A.V. Alexander, MP to Mrs E.B. Leach
   dated 6 April 1942. Courtesy of Admiral of the Fleet Sir Henry Leach, GCB, DL.
Handing Over Certificate 1026 HMS *Prince of Wales* which states 'at sea handed
   over this 31st day of March One thousand nine hundred and forty-one at
   11.50 P.M. o'clock HMS *Prince of Wales* constructed by us for His Majesty's
   Navy. John Harvey. For Messrs Cammel Laird & Co. Ltd. Courtesy of Admiral
   of the Fleet Sir Henry Leach, GCB, DL.

Britannia Royal Naval College
Dartmouth
Devon
TQ6 0HJ

HMS Excellent Museum
Whale Island
Portsmouth
Hants
PO2 8ER

Imperial War Museum
Lambeth Road
London
SE1 6HZ

Naval Historical Branch (Naval Staff)
Ministry of Defence
24 Store, PP20, Main Road
HM Naval Base
Portsmouth
Hants
PO1 3LU

Public Record Office – Admiralty (Adm Series)
Kew

Royal Navy Museum
HM Naval Base (PP66)
Portsmouth
Hants
PO1 3NH

The Royal Archives
The Round Tower
Windsor Castle

INDEX

Index